When I Got You

By
Patricia A. C.

When I Got You by Patricia A. C.

ISBN 978-1-970072-83-9 (Paperback)
ISBN 978-1-970072-84-6 (Hardback)

Printed in the United States of America.

New Leaf Media, LLC
175 S. 3rd Street, Suite 200
Columbus, OH 43215
www.thenewleafmedia.com

CHAPTER 1

Jack

My heart is racing, my head is pounding, and my ears are ringing. Isabel has been lying unconscious now over three hours, but the doctor has assured me that she will be alright even though she has suffered a concussion. She will wake up when her brain has had sufficient rest. It's not that I don't trust the doctor, but I'm so fucking afraid because I've never seen her like this -- hurt, pale in a hospital. I can't comprehend her behaviour either. Just before she passed out and hit her head on the pavement, she called a passer-by by her dead husband's name. I am sure that I heard it right, but I didn't have time to talk to the man she called after because he just disappeared. I asked a couple who were helping me with Isabel if they had seen him, but no one understood me. Argh! Fuck. I need to learn Portuguese. I've been so stupid. I should be able to call an ambulance and explain what happened. Instead, I had to rely on strangers. Well, at least the doctors here speak excellent English.

I look at Isabel again and she is frowning in her sleep. I hear the heartbeat machine she is attached to and it's starting to beep, and I can see her heart rate is increasing quite a bit, too. I got up and pressed the nurse's button and she comes in seconds later.

"What's wrong? Her heart is racing," as my heart is hammering, too.

After the nurse checks, everything seems to be okay. She says Isabel is probably dreaming. I let out a breath that I was holding and clutched Isabel's tiny hand with my larger one.

1

"Babe, please open those gorgeous golden eyes of yours. I need to see them. I need to know you're okay, baby, please," I whispered into our linked hands.

I feel her grip tighten on mine and I lift my head. She is moving her head from side to side now and seems to be in a nightmare.

"Isabel. Isabel, baby, please wake up," I encouraged softly.

"Sam no, no. Please come back." She murmurs.

My heart just stopped. Surely, I didn't hear her right. I mustn't have. Why? Why is she dreaming of Sam? Please God, don't let her have second thoughts about us.

"Sam!" she shouts and bolted upright on the bed.

"Shhh... Baby it's okay. I'm here, I'm here," I say gently.

Isabel brings her hand to her head and hisses slightly. "You hit your head sweetheart, but you'll be okay. I'm here." I said the last part more for myself than for her benefit.

She looks at me with a frightened look. "Where is Sam? I saw him Jack, where is he?" she says looking around, probably expecting to find him here, too. This truly both hurt and scares me. I don't know what to tell her or how to respond.

"Isabel, darling, you hit your head. You're just confused. Rest a little so we can talk later, okay?"

"No, Jack. I saw Sam, I swear," she was holding my hands firmly, and her eyes shed with tears. It fucking hurts seeing her desperate to see her dead husband.

I stood up, feeling confused and hurt and scared for her. I was not sure if it was the concussion or it was the same behaviour she had just before she passed out. I fear it was the latter.

"Okay, look, tell me what happened baby because all I know was one minute we were holding hands talking about our future - all happy and then you just turned to a complete stranger calling for Sam. Then you passed out, fell to the floor while bleeding."

Isabel closed her eyes and took a deep breath, proceeds to lay back on her pillow, and when she opened her eyes, the unshed tears trickled down her sweet pale cheeks.

"You are right. I was so happy walking along the beautiful beach when I felt this...this prickle all over me. And when I looked at this hooded guy passing by, he lifted his eyes to mine. Jack, it was Sam. I know I sound crazy, but it was him," her tears didn't stop falling, and she was clutching her hands so tight to her chest.

I couldn't take it anymore, so I rushed to her side and started to massage her little fists. "It's okay. Just..." my thoughts were all jumbled up and my heart raced. I didn't know how to go from here, how to help her, how to assure her that what she thinks she saw isn't real. I closed my eyes and pull her close to me, resting my forehead to hers as I breathe her scent.

"Okay," I said and continued, "I tried to see the man you are talking about, but he just disappeared, so there is no way for me to know who he was. I don't know what you want me to do, baby. Tell me; tell me what you need, and I will do it for you." I whispered, looking at her beautiful lips.

She let a little choked cry out.

"Jack, I don't know. I just don't know. My head hurts so much, and I cannot stop seeing his eyes looking at me with so much pain in them, so much longing," she said while grabbing my neck and started to sob hard.

I held her tight to me, "Shh. . . It is okay, baby. We will figure it out. Together. Shh."

I never felt so useless as I felt at this very moment. She still loves him. I got jealous over a dead man. She obviously still holds a part of her heart to him, and that completely shatters mine. Even though she told me she would always have him in her heart. I never thought it would hurt so bad to actually see it in her eyes. The desperation and the hope because she saw him again, and I saw it in her eyes that she wants to believe this. God, help me. Don't let me lose her. Not even to a dead man. I do not know what I would do without her and Lara.

When she calmed down, she pulled slowly away, and without looking at me, she said, "I need to rest."

She turned on her side with her eyes closed, "Sleep, baby. I will be outside, making a few phone calls. I will be back in a little while."

I dropped a kiss on her shoulder and left the room. I wanted to move further away but my legs would not move. I dropped to the floor and put my hands on my head. The nurse that came earlier to check on Isabel came rushing and put her hand on my shoulder.

"Sir! Are you all right?"

I looked up, and no words came out, so I just nod.

"You need coffee. Go towards the end of the corridor and turn left, you will see a cafe. Okay?"

But I did not move. "She will be okay, sir. I promise," she said with sympathy in her face. But I wanted to tell her that *I* wouldn't be okay. I know Isabel will be okay from her injury, but emotionally, we both know that we are both feeling broken, and there was very little help. I forced myself to be uptight and started moving towards the cafe, which I found that it was not a cafe but a coffee machine. Once I took a seat by the coffee machine, I called Isabel's mum and then Lizzy.

"Hello?"

"Hi, Lizzy. It's Jack."

"Jack? What's wrong?" she said immediately as if she could tell something was up.

I tried to sound calm and collected, but my voice shook slightly.

"Isabel is in the hospital. She passed out and hit her head on the pavement. But she will be okay. It was just a concussion which the doctor assured me will be okay. . ."

"Okay, but there is something else, isn't there?" she sounded cautious, almost afraid.

"Yes." There was a long pause, then I took a deep breath and told her about Sam.

"We were walking along the beach, talking, laughing, and then there was this man. . . she turned to him while he was passing us and called him Sam. Then she hit the floor fast, unconscious," my voice shook.

"What do you mean Isabel called him Sam? It doesn't make any sense. Are you sure about this Jack?"

"Yes, she woke a little while ago asking for Sam. She truly believes she saw him."

"What the fuck?" she said.

"I don't know what to do. She believes she saw him and I did see a man who disappeared so fast after she has fallen. I didn't have time to look closely; that's why I'm confused. I don't understand how that could even be possible. But Isabel is adamant that she saw him."

"I will fly over as soon as I can. Don't worry. I am sure she is just confused. Everything will be all right, Jack?"

"Yeah, right. I will talk to you later, okay? I have to go now."

"See you, Jack. Jack? She loves you deeply," that was all it took. I put my fist into my mouth.

"Bye," I pressed the end button and slapped the wall.

I rushed to the toilets and sat on the floor and contemplated the fact that Isabel was so adamant about what she saw. I felt so hurt and scared that all thoughts rushed to my mind. What if Sam is alive? What if he comes back? Will Isabel leave me and go back to him? What am I thinking? He cannot be alive, he cannot. I was trying to reason with myself, there is no way he could be alive. He died in a plane crash; the chances of him surviving a plane crash in the middle of the bloody ocean was close to none. Pull yourself together, Jack. This is just a late reaction to our engagement. She is probably subconsciously scared and feeling like she is betraying Sam by marrying me. Yes, that is it. Just get the fuck up, wash your face, drink a coffee, and go be with the woman you love. She needs you now.

I was approaching her room when a man was slipping out of it. I stopped in my tracks. The man turned my way to leave but saw me and stopped. I couldn't see his face because he was wearing a hood, but I knew then that Isabel was right. The man started to walk fast, but I blocked his way.

"Stop, who are you?" the man looked around him and lifted his hood. I recognised him instantly, even though he had grown a beard, and his hair was longer falling over his eyes slightly. It was Sam. Isabel had pictures all around both her houses, and standing in front me was the same man who I saw in those pictures every day.

"It can't be," I whispered.

"I can't stay. I just had to make sure she was okay," he said to me with a hard stare.

"What the. . .? You're supposed to be dead," I said, coming closer to him. Anger started to simmer deep inside me. How could this man be alive and well? He left his wife and daughter, only when she is moving on with her life, he shows up!

"Why?" I asked, grabbing his jumper around the collar?

"I got to go. I can't stay," he said, pulling his hood back into place and pushing my hands away. But I didn't let go.

"No! You are not leaving without an explanation. I need to know why now? If you were alive all this time, why show up now?"

He fixed me with a hard stare as if he was telling me to let him go before he punches my face. But I gave him an equal one. As if he wants to surrender, he exhaled hard and shook his head.

"Meet me tomorrow at *a cabana*, 11 pm. I'll explain what I can, but Isabel can't find out. Now let me go," he growled.

I let go, and he rushed past his shoulder hunched over. I was paralysed twice today as I felt like my world was crumbling down. At least now I know Sam is, in fact, alive and I can deal with it, starting by meeting him and finding out what happened. I straightened up, took a deep breath, and went into Isabel's room. She was fast asleep and more relaxed. Her expression is serene, her cheeks are still pale, but I can see that she is more relaxed now and not dreaming badly again of Sam.

I sat next to her bed and rest my head on the bed, trying to calm my thoughts and figure the best way to deal with Sam.

The next day, Isabel was sent home with painkillers and instructions along, to rest and have someone close by her. I was feeling stronger, too. I decided that I needed to be level-headed on this. I am always so good at solving problems, and very little affects me. But with Isabel, it's different, she makes me feel so small and scared to lose her. But I won't let anything or anyone take her away from me. She is mine.

I asked Isabel's mum to stay over and told her I had a few things to do that night. She found it strange that I would go out at night. It was something out of my character, but I said I need to go for a drive to clear my head, and she didn't press on the issue any longer. Isabel hasn't spoken again about Sam, heck, she hasn't spoken much about anything. She would just reply to any questions asked either with a yes or no, and kept quiet most of the day. I gave her space, not pushing and just being around for anything she needed. At one point, I sat on the bed, and Isabel took my hand so tight with hers, pressed close to her heart, and fell asleep. It made my heart swell with so much love. I know she loves me dearly, but in situations like this, I can't even imagine what is going through her little head.

I arrived at *a cabana* at 10:40 pm, and sat on an outdoor table.

CHAPTER 2

Sam

"Sam, how nice of you to after...what? Five years? Yes, five years to show up."

"I shouldn't have come here. I know."

"Yes, well, it's a little too late for that," his gaze doesn't leave mine.

"Look, I know what you are thinking. How could I leave my wife and daughter and let them think I'm dead. But believe me, I had my reasons."

Jack just nodded and brought a finger to his lips as if he was thinking before responding. "I have been thinking all day for reasons you might have. Memory loss was the only reasonable reason I could think of, but I can see that wasn't it because you seem to recognise Isabel and even myself who you never met before. So I can't think of a good reason enough to leave your wife and child."

That pissed me off. I leaned forward closer to Jack, "Do you think it was easy to leave the woman I loved all my life and my little girl? Do you think I didn't think of them every fucking waking moment, and even when I'm sleeping? I gave up a life of wealth, a gorgeous wife, an amazing daughter, an extraordinary career to keep my family alive." I growled at him.

Jack frowned and became puzzled, "Keep them alive? From whom?"

"From very dangerous people. People that wouldn't hesitate to kill Isabel and Lara even when they have the slightest suspicion," I answered.

Jack's jaw clenched tight. I can see his muscles tensed up and his hand fisted. "Why are these people after you, Sam? What are you involved in?"

I could see Jack was trying hard to maintain his cool. I continued, "I can't say anything further. I can never go back, and Isabel must never see me again." I said feeling dejected and broken.

"You put them in danger, and now you don't want to tell me who these people are?! I need to know so I can protect them. I can't protect them if I don't know who I'm dealing with," he said, glaring at me.

"Jack, you must understand. The people who pose a danger are not after Isabel or Lara. They want me. So if I stay dead, both Isabel and Lara will be safe."

"No! I won't take that risk. You might not care about them enough, but I do. I won't take any risk on their lives, so you are going to fucking tell me who I'm dealing with."

I shook my head. I knew this was a mistake. I should have never come to see him. This idiot doesn't understand. "I have to go. Don't let Isabel find out I'm alive," I started to stand, but Jack seized my harm tight.

"You are not leaving without telling me. Sam, I love them, and if you still have any love left for them, you will tell me who these people are."

I wanted to punch this asshole's face for insinuating twice now I don't love my family, but I also understood him. "Look for *Crown*. They are a British mafia, but I can't tell you any further about them."

I looked around, and I saw a car parked across the road with a man inside. I felt the need to move, so I pulled my hood up, "I got to go." I rushed past Jack, who sat down again. When I passed by the car, the guy inside was speaking Portuguese. He was on the phone, and it seemed he was talking to a girl. I felt nervous, so I walked fast. I was nervously checking my surroundings as I was walking home. I hated feeling tensed all the time.

I was moving around for years. I moved to Portugal only a couple of years ago. Right after the fake accident I was in Brazil for six months and in Ecuador for four months. Venezuela was probably the longest as I stayed there for a year. I realised afterwards that I would make good money if I get into the smuggling business, so I moved to Cuba where I earned the money I needed to come here to Portugal as I always wanted. I now work as a fisherman. Every day is always about hard work to catch fish, but I spend a lot of time in the sea, so it helps to keep myself away from the bad guys. Only a few people know that I'm still alive. They're the ones who passed on information to me about Isabel's life, especially the first time she was seeing Jack. I selfishly thought that she was mine, and noone could have her but me. But the same people who helped me get to know more about Isabel's life were also the ones who made me see that Isabel is truly safe with Jack. With so much influence and power, Isabel and Lara would be protected against anyone who wishes harm to them.

It hurts to see them together as a happy family. I wanted Jack's place so badly, to be able to make Isabel laugh and play with my little girl, Lara, but I know it's impossible. What keeps me going now it's that I know they are safe and will remain so because of Jack.

CHAPTER 3

Isabel

I wake up to find an empty bed. I look at the alarm clock on my bedside table, and it shows 1:30 a.m. Jack must be downstairs, so I pulled the covers off and stepped out of bed slowly. I still feel dizzy and weak. I'm about to descend the stairs when mum comes out of her room.

"Oh querida precisas de alguma coisa?" she is asking if I need anything.

"No mum, go back to sleep, I'm okay, I'm just looking for Jack."

She takes my hand and turns me towards my bedroom again. "Jack said, not to worry, querida. He will be back soon," she says while getting me back to bed.

"He's out? Where? Where did he go at this time, mum?"

Mum pulled the covers close to me, just like when I was small. It was comforting, but my heart was now beating fast. Jack isn't home in the middle of the night. Where could he possibly be?

"Shhh, he will be back soon, agora dorme bem querida," she said while kissing my forehead and left the room. I tried to go back to sleep, but my mind was going through everything, seeing Sam telling Jack about it, and the look of hurt I saw in Jack's eyes and the desperate way he held me. I feel so scared now, all alone. *Has Jack left? No, he would never leave. I know that. Could he be so hurt and went out to clear his head and had an accident? Oh God, he could have had an accident.* I got up and grabbed my mobile, and desperately called him praying for him to answer. On the sixth ring, I hear his quiet voice.

"Isabel, is everything alright?" he asked straight away.

"Yes. I just woke up, and you are not here, and mum said you were gone out."

"I'm just driving back, baby. I just went out for a walk along the beach, that's all," he replied.

I heaved a sigh of relief, "Thank God, you're okay!"

"I'll be there in five minutes sweetheart," he sounded sad. I felt bad because I knew it was because of me.

"Okay see you in a bit then."

Jack ended the call without saying anything else. I laid down and waited for him, but I still didn't feel at ease. I can't rest or relax until I feel Jack in my arms . I hear the front door and sit on the bed cross legged, Jack enters the room and sees me, he stops and don't move any further. I want to say something, do something but my body doesn't obey my mental commands.

"Beautiful" Jack whispers, I almost didn't hear but because the room is so silent I was able to. I smiled a little and Jack started to move towards me, slow, steady strides, my heart quicken. When he is at the bottom of the bed he starts to unbutton his linen navy shirt, slowly, very slowly his hard pecs and abs come into view and I feel a throbbing in my sex, my breath quickens and all I want to do is grab him, take him, touch every inch of his wonderful body, but my body yet again fails me.

Jack must have seen the lust in my eyes because his gaze became heated, his jaw locks and he is a bit faster with his shorts, not as fast as I wanted him to, but still faster. There he stood with his manhood strong and tall, erected, twitching, I wanted to freeze this moment, that look, his lips slightly parted taking me in, ravishing me with his eyes.

"I need you." I hear myself say. The look in his eyes told me that, that is exactly what he needed to hear, I gave him what he wanted without him asking and it tells me how we are made for each other. Then out of the blue Sam's eyes came to my mind and I gasped, Jack didn't miss the change in me, but crawled into bed to me, he cupped my face with both hands and searched my eyes hard, I was scared that he would find guilt in them so I averted ever so slightly my gaze.

"Don't." he says.

"Don't look away from me. Your mine." With that he kissed me passionately, every cell in my body was melting into his kiss, but this wasn't enough I wanted more, I needed more. My hands started to clutch him closer to me, but I felt like I was cheating, this guilt didn't made sense, Sam is dead, I kept saying to myself. *Jack is here and is yours stop thinking of your dead husband, he is not coming back, it was all in your head.* So why can't I stop thinking of him? Jack brought his mouth around my nipple and sucked, licked, worshiped it. He moved to my tummy with wet kisses, he open my legs hard and I gasped, he never been so brusk in his movements, his mouth descended to my sex, sucking so hard on my clits that a cry of pure ecstasy come out of me, he used his tong to enter me and his teeth and upper lip on my clits, the orgasm came so fast and hard I felt my legs trembling. "That's right beautiful, it's me who brings you this pleasure, it's me who will never let go. You are mine and will be mine for the rest of your life, no matter what." He growl into my sex. I wanted to respond, but I couldn't I was feeling split in two and I didn't want to feel like that so I pull his head to me and kissed him deeply, tasting my own juices in his mouth, it made me want more, I wanted him inside me, no I needed him inside me, claiming me as his.

"Fuck me Jack, fuck me hard." I say. I hardly spoke like this, blunt, without inhibition and Jack doesn't hesitate, he plunge into me with a hard thrust, he fucks me hard, slamming into me muttering something which I don't understand, it didn't take long for the feeling of another orgasm to rack my body, but Jack doesn't stop he keeps slamming into me hard, then he takes my asshole, we explored this and I came to enjoy it a lot with Jack, it is still hard as he is so thick but Jack always made me feel good, being careful not to hurt me. Not today, today he is more forceful, he worked my clits at the same time but I can feel him pushing harder.

"Relax baby, I don't want to hurt you." he rasps.

"I need to take your asshole, I can't wait. Not today." He growls. I feel his need to take me, so I relax as much as I can. He rams into me hard and I yelp loudly.

"That's right, it's me who is fucking you in the ass. It's me who will bring you to scream in pleasure once again. Your mine." He whispered into my ear. His words are like fuel to an already raging fire. I can't stop the animalistic sounds that are coming out of my mouth, I never was one to shout while having sex but this need I have to be made his, it's not like all the other times, it's almost an insatiable desire coming from deep in my gut. If I don't give myself to this feeling I won't be his, I will forever be Sam's so I give in, I give all my soul to him, all my heart to him.

I'm his and he is mine. "Oh Jack…yes…I'm…oh" I feel my body starting to go rigid with the orgasm that is building.

"Yes, say it, baby say it." He growls and keeps thrusting hard working my clit with his thick fingers.

"I'm…oh…I'm YOURS…" I shout when the orgasm comes, it rocks my whole body and I feel Jack spill into me too, groaning as he comes deep into my asshole.

"Yes. Yes, you are mine." He whispers in my ear a few moments later. We are breathing hard to catch our breaths, this was a branding and I can say I am branded, Jack has got me and I …I got Jack…but still there is something deep, deep into my soul that calls me a liar, I ignore it and embrace Jack as he withdraws from inside me, we hold each other tight until our breaths and heart beat are normal.

"Jack?"

"Hmm?"

"Where did you go?" this question was met by a long silence. I lifted my eyes to his and they were closed. A feeling of dread came to me then.

"Jack? Where did you go earlier?" I asked again not taking my eyes of his.

"Just for a walk and a drink. That's all." He whispered, tucking a strand of my hair behind my ear.

There was something in his eyes I couldn't read, was he lying to me? He never ever lied.

"Do you trust me Izzy?" he asked looking into my eyes.

"Yes. But..." Jack put a finger on my lips.

"I'm trying to find out what happen to Sam, trust me that I'm looking into it. Just don't ask me how and don't get involved please, I'll tell you everything when I know the facts, ok?" startled by his statement, I couldn't think how he was looking into Sam's death? Can it be possible that he is alive then? Jack saw the wheels turning in my head.

"Hey, hey, Stop, stop thinking too much about this, it's probably nothing but I need to make sure who you saw wasn't him that's all." I could see that he knew more, but he asked me to trust him.

Should I trust him? What am I thinking of course I can trust him, he loves me, he wouldn't do anything to hurt me. I was feeling exhausted so I laid on his chest, curling myself around his firm but comforting body, I nodded as an answer to him and I fell asleep not long after.

I wake up to Jack's kisses on my shoulder.

"Mmmmm...the best way to be waken up."

"Good morning baby. How're you feeling?" I stretch and turn towards Jack.

"Better. My head doesn't hurt any more and I'm hungry, very hungry in fact." I started to kiss his jaw up to his ear and I hear Jack groan.

"Oh yeah? Well I can take care for that for you." he said pulling my hair away from my face. Jack pressed his body over mine pinning me to the bed and started kissing me with fervour, his hands moving down my body going to my breasts, kneading my nipples. I was felling the usual heat Jack always causes in me when I hear a knock at the door.

"Isabel? Querida posso entrar?" oh shit is my mum, I pushed Jack off me so hard he actually slips off the bed.

"Shit. Sorry babe." I say quickly to Jack "Just a minute mama." I answer loudly so my mum could hear. I jump off the bed and put my nighty on which has been discarded from last night's tumble with Jack. Meanwhile Jack almost sprint to the master bathroom. Once I felt a bit more covered up I ask mum to come in.

"Morning mama." I say as she comes in.

"Como te sentes meu bem?" she asks how I feel.

"Better now." She gives me a cheeky grin.

"What a night of passion doesn't cure hey?" she says louder than needed, most likely to let Jack know she knew all about what went on last night.

"Mama!!!!! Stop" I whispered shout.

"Good morning Mrs Silva." Shouted Jack from the bathroom. Mum laughs lightly.

"Breakfast is ready. Also there is a surprise for you downstairs." She says this also louder and in English so she wants Jack to know about the surprise.

After both Jack and I had a quick shower, well, not as quick as it should have been but you know how it is, when having a shower with Jack can never be a very quick one. We came down and I find Lizzy sat at the table scoffing her face with Portuguese fresh pastries.

"Hmmm, this is so good, I can't stop." Says Lizzy to Clara.

"Not even to hug me?" I said. She turn to me and jump to her feet hugging me so tight.

"Of course for you I'll stop anything. How are you?" she says pulling away from me so she could look better at me.

"I'm fine Lizzy."

"Your head" she touched the back of my head.

"It's fine truly." I reassure her. She breathed out a sigh.

"Come sit." She says dragging me to the table. Jack gives Lizzy a kiss on her cheek and they look to each other briefly with an unspoken worry, I didn't let on that I saw their exchange.

After Breakfast we went to get Lara from my uncle's house and we all went to the beach. Jack was most of the time on his phone, he kept saying there was an expected contract he couldn't let it pass but there was something he wasn't telling me. I could feel his uneasiness and whenever he told me something he never looked into my eyes, which is very odd, he is one of those people who always looks you in the eye. At one point he was having a heated conversation on his mobile I could see it clearly from where I was standing, he was waving his hand about and his body seam to be so rigid. Lizzy was behaving strange too, I noticed she kept trying to distract me from Jack.

"Lizzy, something is going on." I said looking to Jack.

"What, with Jack?" she asks.

"Yes. And I have a feeling you know exactly what it is."

"I'm sorry, how would I know if anything was up with Jack?" she asks with a surprised expression. Ok maybe I got it wrong maybe she doesn't know anything, but Lizzy is a good liar so I don't know what to think. Once when we were teenagers we went to a party in a farm of a good friend of ours, before leaving we opened the doors of the sheep barn and they all spill out, now, if wasn't for Lizzy great art of lying we would be in serious trouble, but they actually believed we saw a man opening the barn, so I don't know if she is lying now.

"Are you sure?" I probed "Don't be silly Izzy, Jack is probably with troubles at work."

"No, he would have said if he had any issue at work."

"Well maybe he doesn't want to spoil your holidays." She's probably right. I dropped my eyes from her and let it go.

"You haven't said what actually happen the other day when you fainted and knocked yourself out." She asked. I didn't want to talk about it, because I wanted to forget Sam's eyes. I closed my eyes and gave her a slight shake of my head.

"Hey, hey, it's ok. We don't have to talk about it, but you know I'm here for you right?"

"I know, but you probably going to think I'm losing my mind if I tell you."

"Who me? Thinking you losing your mind? Babe I know you are bonkers already, so whatever you tell me is just another crazy thing you say." That made me chuckle a little. I take a little breath and tell her.

"I was walking with Jack happy as Mary when I saw this man in a grey hoody and there was something off about him, but when he was close enough I could see his eyes and when he lifted them to mine…I saw…it was Sam, Lizzy. I keep telling myself it was all in my head but… I remember his eyes clear as day, he was sad, scared, hurt. Now Jack says he is looking into this but…" I look at her feeling so scared and confused.

"I'm scared Lizzy. What if it's him. You see those things on the telly about people that lost their memory for many, many years, and those who are kidnapped and manage to run."

"Izzy, stop. You can't believe Sam is alive after five years do you?"

"I don't know what to believe anymore."

"Ok let's suppose he still alive, that he lost his memory or whatever, then what?" her question left me speechless.

"You love Jack, Isabel. He's even trying to find out about Sam, that's how much he cares for you and Lara. But if Sam is alive as you starting to believe, what then?" I pull my legs to my chest and hug them close. I look at Lara playing with mum on the sand, making a piano out of wet sand and tears prickle in the back of my eyes.

"I don't know. If God brings him back, surly it means we have a second chance at a family." I whispered.

"But that's the thing Izzy, you already have a second chance at a family, right now, with Jack. You know what I'm saying is true. Can you give Jack up? Can you honestly say you could go back to how things were before?" I'm so confused, my head starts to hurt, I put my hand in my head and feel Jack's hand coming to my cheek.

"What is it Izzy? You're in pain? Sweetheart look at me." I didn't want to look at him because I was so scared he would see that guilt in my eyes again.

"I'm ok honey, just a head acre. Could you get me a drink babe?" I said without moving to look at him.

"Sure, hang on a minute." He left and when I looked up he was actually sprinting across the golden sand into a beach bar to buy me a drink.

"See what I mean? What wouldn't he do for you?" I just nodded but didn't respond.

"Hey, look at me." Lizzy said, so I did.

"Whatever the situation, just know I will be there for you and whatever decision you make will always be the right one."

"This is most likely nothing, it probably is my head playing tricks on me right?"

"Right." She says brighter now.

She is right I can't imagine giving Jack up, but I can't imagine seeing Sam again either and let him go.

CHAPTER 4

Jack

"Richard, I don't want excuses. I just want you to get me the information I requested by the end of today. Got it?" I was fuming mad. Sam is really good at hiding I give him that. On the way home last night, I made a few phone calls and got the best team put together to find people who don't want to be found. There are two groups in this team — one is looking for Sam, and the other is looking for *Crown.*

I found quite a lot of info about the *Crown.* It's the most dangerous mafia established in England, and they have good relations with the Russian mob. Members tend to marry one another, so the bond between the two is stronger. My team doesn't know who their leader is but found a few members who do the *dirty work,* which is a good start i suppose.

With all these evil people around, I guess Sam is *really* good at being impossible to find by the *Crown.*

"Yes, Sir, I'm on it."

I ended the call frustrated. I turned to look to Isabel and notice she has her knees close to her chest. I walked towards her while she clutches her head.

"What is it, Isabel? Are you in pain? Sweetheart, look at me."

She doesn't lookup. I figured she might have talked to Lizzy about the night she fainted.

"I'm ok honey, just a head acre. Could you get me a drink babe?"

"Sure, I'll be right back." I sprinted towards the beach bar. When I returned, I gave her the drink, and she smiled at me and drank the Iced Tea.

"Feeling better?" I asked.

"A little. Thank you," Isabel grabs my hand that is resting on her knee and kisses it.

She's in pain. The kind of pain that she wants to believe that Sam is alive. But I can sense deep down that she already knows the truth. I don't know what to do. Should I just tell her everything I know or just hold on until I know where Sam is and tell her? I never kept anything from her before and never lied either. Yet I find myself doing so now.

"You should be resting, Isabel," I said, pressing my right hand against her cheek. "Let us head home," I continued. I wanted to show Isabel around and spend the day lying here on the beach and then have dinner in a restaurant, but i can see she's not well.

"I'll be fine, honey," she says, but I can see how tired she is.

"I'll speak to Tiago and Lucia if they don't mind spending the day with Lizzy. You need to rest, you are not well. Would that be fine?" I asked.

"Of course not. I was going to suggest that to Izzy. I will have Lara come over, too. I want to spend time with my god-daughter, and this is a perfect time to do that," Lizzy said, looking to Izzy.

"Fine. That's not fair, you know. It's two against one," Isabel replied.

I smiled at both of them. "Let's go, Isabel," grabbing her hand and lifted her into my arms, carrying her to the car.

"I don't need to be carried. I can walk."

"I know, but I love to carry you in my arms. Besides, I need to practice for the *big day*. If you know what I mean."

She laughed and it helped lifting off a bit of tension from her body.

"Who are those men?" she asks, noticing the two men next to our car.

"Isabel meet Pedro, our driver, and Alex." She shakes both men›s hands and looks at me for further explanation, but I don't give any.

When we are inside the car, she turns to me, "Okay, why do we have a driver?" She whispers.

"Because I can afford one, and we are both too tired to drive around. I should have had a driver from the beginning anyway." I said, trying to sound nonchalant.

"Hmm... and Alex? Who is he?" At the mention of his name, Alex looked over his shoulder and smiled at Isabel.

"Well, Alex is our bodyguard. Before you say anything, Alex has worked for my father for over three years previously. That is why I chose him to be our bodyguard. You know I'm the CEO of one of the biggest recording companies in the world, so there are a lot more risks. I tried to be discreet about it, and it worked. You never noticed his presence even though he has been with us for almost a year now."

"How come I never saw him?" she asked me, surprised by my admission.

"As I said, I wanted it to be a hundred percent discreet."

"So what changed now?" she asked.

Again I tried to sound nonchalant, "You will be my wife, and I thought you should meet the team. There are a few others, but they are busy at the moment."

She looked at me with such a surprised look in her cute face. I bring my thumb to her slightly parted lips. "Don't worry, honey. It doesn't change anything."

She frowned and looked out the window, thinking. I didn't want to overwhelm her, but after the appearance of Sam, everything has changed. It's true Alex is my bodyguard, and a few others are Isabel and Lara's security, but I made sure they weren't noticeable. Holidays came, and I asked them to go on vacation, even the security team. I thought it was the right decision at first, but it was the stupidest decision I have ever made, after learning about Sam I asked them back ASAP.

Isabel didn't utter a single word until we got inside the house. She turned slowly to me, and I knew she wasn't happy.

"You said there are others, but they are busy. Doing what exactly?" she asked persistently.

I knew I couldn't escape her, "Remember I asked you to trust me? Well, just trust me on this, okay? The only thing you need to know at this moment is that they are good at what they do, and they are willing to protect us with their lives if need be."

"Jack, you are scaring me. What are they protecting us from?" she asked, clutching both her hands to her chest.

"Isabel, you don't have to be scared. All of these are purely a precaution. I'm well known worldwide, but this comes with dangers, too. I hope you understand that this is something you have to be accustomed to." I could see in her eyes that she was having a hard time accepting everything I said.

"I get that, yes. But there is something I can't explain why I feel this is wrong. Just promise me you will tell me everything, even if we are in danger, I need to know."

"I promise. I will tell you anything you need to know." I see her hesitation in believing me in her eyes. She knows I'm holding something back purposely but didn' press on the issue.

I received a call from my team that they found Sam onboard on a fisherman's boat. They said Sam works for a small-time family business and goes away for fishing for weeks up to months. No one knows about his story except that he is from Venezuela. At least that is what he likes anybody to think. Sam is smart as he never utters anything in English, so people would believe that he came from far away. But my team was able to track him despite the difficulty of finding him.

Now that I know where he is, I don't really know what to do next. Should I tell Isabel, or should I hold this information from her? If I tell her, there is a possibility I may lose her, putting her in danger, for which I can't let happen. She won't forgive me if she finds out herself either. I have never been so confused right now. I gripped on my phone while looking at Isabel through the patio doors laying down on a lounger under the sun with the umbrella giving her shade, her eyes closed and peaceful, unaware of the battle inside my head and heart. I need to speak to someone about this like, Ian. Someone whom I can trust. Ian has been a good friend to me for many years. He's in a good place right now with his new girlfriend, but at the same time, I don't want him to be caught in the middle of this issue.

When Lizzy returned from her day with Lara and Isabel's cousins, I tucked Lara in, read her a story that she loves the most.

On my way back on the corridor, I stumbled upon Lizzy and stopped her on her way to bed, "Lizzy, I need to speak to you. Do you have a minute?" She nodded and followed me to the study room closing the door behind. I waited until she finally settles into her seat, "I will be straightforward. Sam is alive," I paused to give her time to digest and continued, "On the day I called you from the hospital when I returned to Isabel's room, I saw a man coming out, and it was Sam. He has grown a beard and hair, but I recognised and confronted him. He agreed to meet with me yesterday, and he told me he had to disappear to protect Isabel and Lara's lives. I don't want you to know everything because it could put you in danger, too. I had put a specialised team with my security team in search of answers. They know where Sam is, and I want to tell Isabel about it, but this might put her and Lara in danger."

"Wait a minute will you?" Lizzy says as she is trying to wrap her head around what I told her. "Sam is alive. He turns up after five years and says he had disappeared to protect Isabel and Lara. So what changed?" She continued, "Why show up now?"

I heaved a sigh and rested back into the chair, "He said it was a mistake to show up, and he doesn't want me to tell Isabel he's alive. I understand his point, but I know Isabel, and she knows she saw him, and she won't let that go. How can I tell the woman I love that her husband is alive?" I said, clutching my hands into fists and closing my eyes briefly.

"Why not tell her Jack? She loves you. But you know you will lose her forever if she finds this out from someone else. You know I'm right. Tell her that Sam is alive," Lizzy said.

"What?!" came a voice from the door.

My eyes meet with Isabel's and the way she looks at me. She was so hurt and confused. I jumped on my feet and shouted in surprise, "Isabel!"

CHAPTER 5

Isabel

I was in bed waiting for Jack, but he was taking too long. He was supposed to tuck Lara in and come to bed, but it has been an hour. I got up from bed, stopped in Lara's room just to check that he hadn't fallen asleep with her, but he wasn't there. So I went downstairs, and on my way to the kitchen, I thought I heard voices coming from the study room, so I walked towards it. My tummy tightened upon hearing Jack and Lizzy's voices. I thought I would be jealous, but it hit me that they were talking something shocking behind closed doors. As I opened the door, what I heard was even more disturbing than what was in my head a minute ago.

"Why not tell her Jack? She loves you. But you know you will lose her forever if she finds this out from someone else. You know I'm right. Tell her that Sam is alive," Lizzy said.

"What?!" I couldn't bring myself to process what I have just heard. Sam is alive. I had a hunch that this was true, but hearing it out loud didn't make it easier to grasp. And Jack knew, and he didn't bother telling me. Now it made all sense - his behaviour of being possessive, the constant hiding of infor-mation, and asking me to trust him, his lack of eye contact overtime he spoke to me. I looked into his eyes as he jumped on his feet and came towards me, and I knew he was scared. It was the first time I saw him having that kind of look.

"How long did you know about this?" I managed to choke out over the lump in my throat.

"Since the day you were in the hospital. He came over while I pop out to make a few phone calls, and when I returned, he was just leaving your room," he said as his voice shakes.

I nodded slightly, trying not to cry. *I will not cry.* I tell myself.

"He agreed to meet me and tell me why he disappeared," Jack said.

"You met him last night?" I said, not looking away from his eyes.

He simply nodded, and I saw him gulping. I closed the door and rested against it. Jack moved to hold me, but I put my hand in front of him, signalling him to stop. He stopped and looked hurt.

"I don't know what to say. I need to put my thoughts together," I turned my eyes to Lizzy, "You knew, too?" I asked her.

"I just found out Isabel, I swear," she said, moving towards me. She hugged me, and I let her stand close to me. I was surprised I was not crying like I finally had the answer I was waiting for all this time. I still have many questions unanswered though.

I straightened up and untangled myself from Lizzy. "Lizzy, can you leave Jack and me for a minute?" she understood and nodded.

Before she left, she kissed me on my cheek and whispered to my ear, "Remember what we talked about earlier."

Earlier she asked me what do I do if Sam was alive. Would I let go of Jack? I pushed that thought to the back of my mind. At this moment, I needed to concentrate on finding out about everything.

I strode past Jack and sat on the chair adjacent to the desk and waited for him to sit where he was before. I lifted my head and looked him into his Green eyes, determined to find out about everything he knows. "Start talking and don't leave any details out."

He was quiet for a while, body tense, and his eyes were looking at me, searching for something that I don't know. He sighed and started, "At the hospital, you were in bits, telling me you saw Sam. I didn't know what to make of it first. First, I thought you had some kind of delayed guilt feelings and second thoughts of marrying me. But when I came back to the room and saw Sam, standing there in front of me. I was confused, angry, furious that he left you and Lara all these years. I confronted him, and he agreed to meet me. I didn't tell you because you weren't okay, both physically and mentally, at that time."

I didn't say anything, so he continued, "He has grown a beard and hair. He walks hunched over, and I knew there was something seriously wrong with him. He wouldn't have left his life to become what he is now."

"And what is he now exactly?" I asked.

"He is a fisherman. As we speak, he's at sea, probably trying to keep his identity hidden. He lives in an old fisherman's home near to where he is working. Yesterday, when I met him, he told me he had to disappear to save you and Lara's lives. He refused to tell me anything further as there were people after him. People that kill for a hobby so to speak. They are with the English Mafia..." he stopped because he saw the fear in my eyes.

"Isabel, no one will hurt you or Lara. I promise you that. I will never let anything happen to either of you, do you understand me?" he says with determination.

I believe him. I know he would never let anything happen to us. I was not scared for myself. I was afraid for Sam. *Why wouldn't he tell me that he was in trouble? We could have worked something out without leaving us.* Knowing he left without even talking to me about it hurts even more.

"Go on," I said.

"I have a team who have been tirelessly searching for answers about this English Mafia. It's not good, though. They are very close to the Russian Mob making their alliances and connections even stronger than before. I'm afraid I couldn't yet get more information, but my team is working day and night to find out more and shed some light on why Sam would be involved with them."

"Okay so what's next?" I asked.

He frowned, not understanding what I mean by it.

"What are you going to do next when the information you have been waiting for comes? What do you intend to do about it?" that thrown him off.

"I don't know. I rely on both the head of the teams, Richard and Alex to give me their input and the best course of action, of course. I don't have a plan, Isabel. Not at this point. I need all the information first and plan from there. But my priority is you and Lara's safety."

"That makes sense," I replied.

"What are you going to do now that you know Sam's alive?" he said in a small voice, clasping his hands tight on top of the desk.

I thought about it for a minute before answering.

"He's at sea at the moment, correct?"

"Yes," he answered.

"Is there any way you will know when he comes back home?"

"Yes, my team is following his every move."

I frowned at that statement believing they couldn't do that, "At sea?"

"Yes, when you have the money, you can have eyes everywhere," he replied.

"How long did it take for you to find him?"

"24 hours."

"That means the Mafia can find him faster than you. They have more resources than you do," I said, starting to panic.

"My team is special, quick on their feet, and agile. They found Sam because of his description. Otherwise, it would be close to impossible to find him. Don't forget that everyone thinks he's dead."

That made me feel somewhat better. "Can you please tell me when he will be back? I want to speak to him."

Jack started to shake his head, and before he refused, I went on, "Jack I need to speak to him. I need to hear this from him. He left Lara and me without explanation, without telling me he was in trouble. I need to speak to him. Please."

His eyes soften, and he nodded, "Fine. I will let you know when he's back."

I sink further into the chair, feeling exhausted and completely drained from all of this.

"You should go to bed, darling," he whispered. Only then I realised he had moved from behind his desk and crouched next to me.

I looked into his eyes and see everything — pain, confusion, and afraid. I placed my hands on his cheeks, and he closes his eyes, leaning into my touch.

"Thank you," I tell him. Nothing more I could say for now. Nothing that I could say would show him how grateful I am for what he's doing. He kissed my forehead, gets up, and turns towards the window.

I slowly get up and leave him be. He needs his space, and so do I. I feel numb as I get in bed. I close my eyes and forget everything that happen tonight as I surprisingly fell asleep fast. I didn't have dreams tonight, nor bad nor good. I didn't dream of anything at all.

The next day, I woke up without Jack beside me. I knew he hadn't been to bed because his side was neat. Sadness dawned on me, knowing he was still hurting, and it was all because of me. *No, it isn't because of me. It's Sam's fault.* I felt angry now; he left us and in so much pain. *How could he possibly leave our little girl? I won't forgive him for abandoning us. He promised 'till death do us apart' and lied.*

I rushed to the bathroom to get ready. I need to see Jack and feel his arms around me. I was so confused yesterday, but today, I feel better. I'm Jack's, and he is mine. He's the only one for me, the only one who will never leave, and the only one who will do the right thing without having to give us up.

As I descend the stairs, I realised how much I needed Jack at this moment. I looked all around the house, but there was no Jack or Lara for that matter.

"Clara, have you seen Jack this morning?" Clara was in the laundry room, folding bedsheets when I walked in a rush.

"Yes, he took Lara for breakfast, and they were going to the park. You know the one with the cars for children."

"Ah, one of Lara's favourite places." My heart couldn't take it anymore. Jack, in the midst of all of this, put us first.

"He said something about being back by lunchtime and asked if you could be ready. He would like to take you somewhere."

See, this is what I mean. I saw how hurt Jack felt yesterday, and yet, he's sticking around no matter what. Clara must have noticed how my eyes sparkled with unshed tears.

"Oh, *querida*. What is it? I have noticed Jack was quiet, and now you are about to cry. Did you fight?" Clara left what she was doing and grabbed both of my hands.

"No, no. It's complicated."

"Are you having second thoughts about the engagement?" she asked.

I let out a loud sigh, "No. I know he's the right one. There are just a few issues we need to sort out, that's all."

Clara gave me a hug and whispered, "He loves both you and Lara more than anything. Anyone can see that a mile away. No matter what is going on, just remember you are loved by a man who would do anything for you."

I nodded because I knew all that, but Clara doesn't know about the issues that weren't simple to solve. I wanted Jack, and I knew he is the one for me. *Yes, I will be marrying Jack. But... No, Isabel. There are no buts. Sam made you suffer. He left you and Lara, and he broke the promise he made.*

So I got ready for Jack, feeling giddy. My nerves were all over the place. I looked at myself in the mirror. I wasn't sure where Jack was going to take me, so I went casual chic — wearing a designer Sky Blue jumpsuit, with a deep V neckline. I had a custom-made flower platform shoes and a clutch that matches. I had my hair in waves pulled to the side with a Blue flower clip. My make-up was simple and just a bit of mascara and eyeliner and a pink lip gloss. I also had my Chanel studs that Jack gave me on my birthday, and the diamond bracelet he gave me on Lara's birthday. He said Lara's birthday wasn't only her day but mine, too, since it was me who brought her to this world, and I deserve to be appreciated. I cannot help but think that this is the guy I'm going to get married to.

I was so focused on my thoughts that I didn't hear him until he was behind me, and his eyes were looking at me from head to toe in the mirror reflection.

"Perfection!" was the only thing he said.

I gave him a small smile and turned to him. I couldn't contain myself, so I grabbed his face with both my hands and kissed him. Jack was stunned for a moment, but it didn't take long. His hands came around my lower my back and pulled me into him. We were lost in that heated kiss, but Jack slowly ended the kiss, resting his forehead to mine. Our breaths were coming in pants, and I felt my insides on fire. I wanted more of him.

"Well, that was certainly a very lovely 'hello'," he said with that smirk of his I so much adore.

"It could always be better," I said breathlessly.

Jack chuckled a little, shaking his head and looking into my eyes. His beautiful Green eyes still do what they did to me a year ago. My heart rate goes up like a racing car at its maximum speed, to which he interrupted, "I think you need to *uhm,* retouch your make-up."

I looked at myself, and in fact, he was right. We both laughed, and soon, he had me inside the car with Pedro driving, and Alex in the front seat. I was starting to feel comfortable with having someone watching us. Even though there was always someone watching us before that, I didn't know. I guess there is a lot I don't know about Jack because he is always on the phone speaking about investments, and oil reef somewhere in the Atlantic. When the car came to a stop, I looked through the window and realised we were in the middle of a vineyard.

"Where are we?" I looked at Jack, and he had a grin on that beautiful face of his. Every time he gives me that grin, it reminds me of the day, he was still my boss, and all the memories came rushing back, making my heart leap faster.

We came a long way with ups and downs, and now I have him, I want to give myself all to him — the man that do anything and everything for me and my little girl, Lara.

"I want you to meet someone," Jack said.

"Okaaay, that doesn't explain where we are," I said, trying to get more information.

"So, I know you always liked to have your business, and as you are such a great decorator with an extraordinary eye for detail, I saw this place and thought you could turn it into a rural hotel for me."

I was staring at him still not understanding what he meant.

"What I'm trying to say is that we have talked about you wanting to build a home design business, right?"

"Yes, when Lara is in high school, that's what I would do. But she's still in Juniors..." I said.

"Okay, I get that, and I know between her school, her career and you working for me it can be a lot, but with a little help from me you could start your venture early. What a better way to start with one of my projects. You could start to build a portfolio with some of my recent investments, and I have lots of contacts, as I have told you before, who would love to work with you."

Wow, I could not stop admiring this man. He did everything for me. I was sure he bought this place on purpose so I could start my business. "I... I... don't know what to say," I said quietly.

Jack took my hand and brought it to his lips, pressing hard. "Say, you will do it. Say you will follow your dreams and start the business you always wanted."

"Jack, you cannot possibly work around Lara's schedule. You have so much responsibility, and your workload is excessive as someone running a company the size of yours. You took the company on only just over a year, and I know there is still a lot of work to be done with the new changes you are implementing. You can't focus as well on Lara's schedule." I know he wants to give everything to me, but there is no way he can take on that.

"Isabel, can you please trust me that I have everything under control, and when I tell you I will help with Lara, I mean it?"

"Jack, I trust you, I do. But it will affect your career, and I can't have that. I'm happy to wait for the right time to start my venture. My family is more important than anything."

Jack smiled and went on, "I know, and that is one of the many things I love about you. But I have all set up already. I have been quite busy the last year, and while we are here, I still made sure my plan was always on course." He continued, "I now have three PAs, and you are not one of them. Not that I don't want you as my PA; you have been the best PA I have worked with. But I want you to succeed in what you were born to do. You are a leader, baby, and you should have your company." "I also have an expert investment broker who takes care of all my investments outside the company, and he deals with everything for me. It's true, I'm the CEO of the company, but I'm not the only one who is responsible for the company. Our board members are all competent and hard-working people who are all hands-on with the projects I set out in the company," he carried on, "I have done the hard work I needed. I now distribute the tasks, and the only thing that I must take on myself are events that I need to attend with you by my side as always and make sure we have all the best artists in the world under our belt."

Okay, and he thinks that isn't a lot. "Jack, that is still a lot of work plus all this trouble with…"

"Can we just go in and look around? They will also be serving late lunch, and we will be trying their new wine. I know, I know that you don't drink, but they have non-alcoholic wine here, too."

Fuck, this man thinks of everything. I felt my eyes burn a little with emotion, and I just nodded.

We were at a vast farm vineyard. The building itself is stone-built, thus old, distributed into two floors, and a huge stone barn where they brew all their wine. It's so beautiful and so rustic. There is so much you can do here. I was lost with the ideas that kept popping into my head, the colours that could be used, and the possibilities to expand using lots of glass to bring the outdoor-indoor feel. I was telling Jack about my ideas, and I didn't even realise that he was writing things down until a lady came in and introduced herself.

"Hello, my name is Amelia Faria."

"Hi there! I'm Isabel and this is Jack," I replied, still puzzled about Jack taking notes.

"So, I believe your family is Portuguese?" she asked with a big smile. She seems so friendly and so upbeat it made me smile, too.

"Yes, we are from not far. Can I just say your English is excellent!" I complimented her.

"Oh, thank you! I worked for a few years in England when I was younger, so I picked up a few things along the way."

We chatted a bit, getting to know each other, but Jack kept quiet, he would respond when I asked something, and he would smile at the right time, but I didn't understand why he was so quiet. He let me lead, asking all the questions I thought he would need to know, making sure that I covered everything from the local businesses they were involved to reasons why they were selling it. Even what their financial situation was at this point.

I also asked about legal planning permission restrictions in the area. Amelia was well-organised, and she knew all the answers to my questions without hesitation.

"An excellent friend of mine made you a beautiful lunch outside in the patio near the water stream. So I hope you guys enjoy it. Here's my card. I'm leaving you now, but please feel free to stay as long as you want. You will see the farm's staff moving around, going on with their chores. Ask any questions to them. They are all capable of answering and assisting you," Amelia said, taking us to where our table awaits us with the girl in a waiters uniform beside it.

"Hello, my name is Sandra. I'm your food server. If you need anything, you can call me, and I will come to assist you."

Wow, how much is Jack paying these people, I wonder.

I waited for our food to come before speaking to Jack. "Okay, so I'm totally confused here. I thought you wanted to buy this place, and you have been quiet the entire time we were here."

Jack laughed lightly, "Yes, you are completely right. I let you lead; as I said when we were in the car, you were born to lead, Isabel."

So he did this on purpose.

"I knew you would love this place, and I was right. The way you envision this place made me want to come and stay here already. You not only have a gift for interior design, but you also know what property development is all about. You can turn something that is almost run down into something spectacular. The ideas you have, I had to write them down. If you doubt your skill, I needed to show you. I believe you can have a business not only on interior design but property development too, hence, I'm buying this place for you to do whatever you want. It's yours."

I was completely surprised. This couldn't be true.

"What? No," I said, shaking my head. "I can't possibly take that. You buy it, yes, and I will help you with developing it into a five-star rural hotel spa, but I wouldn't take ownership of it. I don't even know what to do with it once it has been completed. Jack, I'm so thankful for what you want to do. I will love it if you keep it as one of your investments while I help you transforming this whole thing ready for you to run it.

"So, you mean we could be partners?" Jack said with a cheeky grin

"Well, no. If we were to be partners, I would have to put some capital as well," I fired back, which made Jack laugh.

"Fine. I will buy the damn thing, and you transform it into what you have in mind. I don't need any input. Whatever you need or want to do to the place, just do it, I'll get an agent take care of the running of he place once is ready." Jack said, grabbing both my hands.

"You know I will have to fly over at least once a week to keep up with the progress, right?"

"It's a good thing we have a private jet," he said cheekily.

How could I be so lucky? Moments like this, I didn't even know if I deserve this man.

"I guess I can travel on Fridays, which means I wouldn't have to take a lot of time from work to help with Lara. I could also change her schedule to make sure there are no activities after school. We would fly at 5 p.m. and be here at 7 p.m. This would give me enough time to have meetings at 8 p.m. Saturdays would be to source out materials, and Sundays I would be back and it would be our family day," I said excitingly.

Everything seems to fit in. I was getting excited that this could actually work.

"See, what did I tell you? You were born to lead. I will support you as much as I can, and we deal with anything that eventually comes our way," he said.

My heart can't contain the love I feel for this man. I leaned in and kissed him, caressing his cheek with one hand and grabbing his shirt with the other. We broke our sweet kiss with a clearing of our throats as Sandra walked in.

"How was the food? Everything to your liking?" said Sandra.

"It was ravishing," said Jack, looking at me with a grin.

I was blushing, probably the darkest shade of red I ever had. "Yes, it was lovely. Thank you, Sandra."

She smiled at us, and just before leaving with the empty dishes, she winked at me, which made me chuckle a little.

Jack and I walked a little through the vineyard. I ruined my beautiful shoes, but it was so worth it. We talked about the plans for the place, and how we could work around our schedules.

Everything was settled, and by the time we got to the car, Jack got a phone call. His mood suddenly changed, which tells me that it was extremely serious. I tried not to ask him about it, but I'm too nosy, and I couldn't wait.

"What was that about?" I tried to sound uninterested.

He looked at me, pressing his lips together, and I saw his jaw ticking, which didn't help at all.

"Is something wrong?" I asked.

He averted his eyes while he spoke, "Sam will be *home* in two days."

I looked down at my hands, and my vision caught Jack clenching his first on his lap. I didn't know how I felt. My heart was racing like a horse, my hands were getting sweaty, and my mouth was dry. I was panting, and I looked at Jack, but he wasn't looking my way. I knew why. He was scared, and I couldn't blame him. He knows I love him, but I have also loved my husband, Sam. Even when I had doubts about Jack before, today, Jack puts his best foot forward that mine and Lara's interests are more important than anything else.

I slowly reached out to his clenched fists and looked straight into his eyes. We were both silent, but I was trying to let him see my love for him.

"Fuck," he said, dragging me to him and hugging me so tight that my chest had little room to breathe.

I appreciated it. I needed this from him.

"I don't want to lose you," he whispered in my ear.

"I know," I said. I wanted to assure Jack that he wouldn't lose me, but there is something that is holding me back. How sure am I that he wouldn't lose me?

"Will you come with me?" I know I'm selfish, but I need Jack to level my emotions and thoughts, he is always the anchor I need.

He let go and looked me into my eyes. "Always. I'll go to hell and back with you, for you," he said with such determination. His eyes were bloody dark, and they almost looked, Black. I love all the shades of his eyes. They were the door to his soul. They change shades depending on his emotions, and there isn't one shade that wouldn't take my breath away.

I wanted to spend a day with Lara, just us two. So that is what we did the following day. I knew Jack had a lot of work to do anyway. The company needed him, and I know we will have to leave soon. But I needed to put this problem with Sam to rest before leaving. I have no idea what will I say to him, or what will happen, but something will definitely have to be done. He's committing a crime, and he's missing a lot on his daughter growing up.

"Mummy, are you okay?" Lara asked with concern etched on her beautiful face.

"Yes, honey. I'm fine," I could tell she didn't believe me, so I went on further, "There are a few things mummy has to deal with, but nothing to worry yourself with, sweet pea."

"Okay. I think I can tell you now," Lara started to say. "My new album is going to be out on the 1st of September," she said, beaming at me.

Wow, my little girl has done it. She worked hard this past year, working with some of the most famous artists, both in classical and pop genres. Her adaptations to different music are exceptional, and her lyrical writing is actually quite good; that is why a few artists adopted her lyrics with her playing and singing, too.

"That's wonderful, sweet pea. I'm so proud of you!" I gave her a tight hug, and she pulled back, looking a little sad.

"What is it, baby?" I asked with concern.

"Do you... do you think dad would be proud, too? I mean, I know Jack is super proud because he tells me all the time how amazing I am. But..."

This made me suddenly cry. "Oh, mummy! I'm sorry. I didn't mean to," she said, hugging my waist.

"It's okay, sweet pea. Yes, I'm sure your dad would be very proud of you," I managed to say with such difficulty.

I was starting to sob now, and I noticed a few people in the park where we were walking were giving me concerned looks. I tried to pull myself together, but I felt hurt at the injustice my little girl is experiencing, having her dad not being around whom she can share her happiness.

I realised Sam is so stupid. How could he do this to our little girl? He robbed her of having a father to share her successes. Bastard.

"Let us sit first," I said to Lara guiding her to a bench.

"You feel better, mummy?" she asked looking at me with so much concern.

"Yes, darling. All better now. I'm sorry. I'm just feeling a little emotional, that's all."

She frowned and asked, "Why?"

Why did I have to say that? What should I tell her?

"Do you remember the time when you learned about the *month thing* in school? It's that time for mummy."

"Ohhhh, I get it now. That's okay, mummy. I won't tell anyone," she whispered back to me, making me laugh a little.

"Ready for ice cream?" I asked, hoping to change the subject.

"Oh yeah!" she jumped off the bench so fast.

The rest of the day went great. We went shopping and went to a local market where we bought so many things. We struggled to carry them, even with Alex, who was carrying lots of bags, all of our hands were full.

"Jesus, did you buy a whole shop?" Lizzy said when we arrived home.

"We went to the market, Aunt Lizzy," said Lara jumping up and down.

"You should have seen it. It has everything you want. There were even puppies and kittens, and ducks, chickens, everything you can think of. Mummy said we could go back next week if we're still here."

Lizzy looked at me with a question in her eyes. I averted my eyes.

"I thought I heard a bird chirping around," said Jack coming from the study room.

"Jack!" Lara exclaimed and ran to Jack. He scooped her up, spinner her around. "We got a few things for you from the market. Mummy said you wouldn't want anything from there, but I made her buy it."

"You didn't make me do anything. I just thought Jack could have something different to remember Portugal," I said.

"Did you now? And what did you get me exactly?" Jack said.

"I will show you later," I said, trying to sound sexy, which made Lara laugh.

"We got you boxer shorts, socks, a Portugal football kit, and..." Lara puts the finger on her chin as if thinking of anything else. "Oh, and a keyring!"

"Wow, I must have been good to get all of those goodies," he told her, trying to sound surprised.

Lara laughed and gave him a kiss on the cheek.

"Dinner is ready!" Clara shouted from the kitchen.

"We just got here on time, how good is that?" I said, turning towards the kitchen. Only when I got to the kitchen did I see how many people were there.

"Ola!" Everyone said at the same time. All my uncles and aunties were there, and some of my cousins, too.

"*Anda querida senta-te?*" My mum asked me to sit. I was really surprised she and everyone were here.

"Did something happen?" I asked my mum quietly.

"No *filha*. Jack thought you need your family around," she whispered in English, so my uncle beside her couldn't understand.

I looked at Jack, who was going to take a seat next to me. He was smiling at me — the kind of smile that made him look just like his father. Every day, he does something for me, like making me feel important. I held his hand and thanked him with a kiss on the cheek.

The dinner went on with a lot of laughter from my Portuguese family. My cousin even started playing *concertina* while my uncles battle it out through singing. It was such a happy time that made me forget the issues Jack and I are surrounded by.

CHAPTER 6

Jack

Seeing Isabel happy - laughing, singing, and dancing, it was what I needed. I love this woman more than life itself. I sat there looking at her wondering how this woman brought light into my life, how she not only gave me this year with her but also with her little girl. They are such beautiful people - if only they knew how much I loved them both.

"Come on, Jack. Come dance!" called Lizzy.

"Oh, no. I'm fine here watching," I replied.

"That isn't fair. Isabel made me dance, so you have, too!"

"Yes, come on, baby. I know how good you dance," Isabel said with a cheeky smile.

"Well, this is different, blimey me. I don't think I can dance that." Portuguese dance looks difficult with various and complicated steps, which I'm sure that I would look foolish if I tried. But I should have guessed that Lara would come rushing to me and got me up from the seat in a few seconds. I wasn't able to say no to her.

By the time all the family went home. Lara was asleep on the sofa, and I felt like all the issues we have been facing were forgotten.

"I'll tuck her in," I whispered to Isabel, picking up Lara gently, trying not to wake her.

"I'll be up in a little while. I just need to switch on the dishwasher and close up downstairs," she whispered back.

I could see that the happiness started to leave slowly her eyes replaced by immense sadness of the issues we are facing. I hate to see her like that, but I didn't say anything about it, so I wouldn't aggravate her.

I was looking for Isabel around the house after tucking Lara in because she was taking too long. She wasn't anywhere. I started to panic, going up and down the stairs checking each room, and I stumbled upon fainting light under a door. It was the bedroom she shared with Sam. It made me pause for a second, tightening in my heart like someone was actually grabbing my heart and squeezing. I lift my fist to knock on the door, but I hesitated for a moment. *What if she doesn't want me here? What if she is thinking being with me is a mistake? Oh God, she's going to leave me, isn't she?*

Before, I didn't mind knowing she still had a part of her heart that belonged to Sam because I thought he was dead. Now that he is completely alive, I'm worried about how we are going to fill our lives with memories and moments onwards. Isabel can still create memories and important moments with Sam again. What is our year of relationship worth compared to a lifetime and a daughter they share? *What am I doing? Why am I making this more complicated than it is? Isabel should have what she needs, and that isn't me. Sam is her husband, and she needs him. He's the father of her daughter, Lara, the little girl I adore. They aren't mine, and they will never truly be mine.*

As this realisation hits me, I got completely exhausted and lost my balance, so I leaned my forehead on the wall next to the door. I wanted to cry. Since I met Isabel, I feel like crying a few times. But I know where I stand now. She belongs to Sam.

I straightened up, took a deep breath, and knocked on the door, determined to get this over with.

"Come in," Isabel said in a small voice. I opened the door, and she is sat on the bed holding something.

I approached and sat next to her, looking at the picture frame she was holding. It was her wedding picture of her and Sam. My chest tightened, but I averted my gaze a moment to pull myself together.

Isabel grabbed my hand, bringing it to her lips. I gently pulled my hand out of her reach and faced the large sliding doors with my hands fisted inside my shorts' pockets.

"Isabel, I think we need to talk," I spoke while not facing her.

"About what?" she asked in a small strained voice.

I closed my eyes briefly and turned to her. "I'm flying back home tomorrow."

She frowned, "Jack, I'm meeting Sam tomorrow."

I nodded, acknowledging what she said. "Yes, I know I said I would be there with you, but..." I swallowed hard before continuing," I'm leaving."

"What do you mean *you are leaving*? Can't you wait so we can all fly home together after the meeting?"

She didn't understand what I meant. I pinched the bridge of my nose, "No, Isabel. I'm leaving alone. You need to be here... with Sam."

She dropped the picture frame and stepped forward, rushing towards me. "What are you talking about? You are not leaving without Lara and me."

It was becoming difficult for me, so I looked into her eyes and said, "I know I said I would never leave you, but Isabel, you must see the truth that Sam is your husband, the father of your wonderful daughter. Even if we are together, it doesn't change the fact that he is alive, and you belong to him."

Her eyes started to shed with tears. I stopped because I saw the pain in her eyes, which was also the exact feeling I have.

"I'm yours, remember? I'm here, and you are here. This is the right thing," she said, putting a hand over my chest.

But I shook my head, "No, the right thing is the three of you." I put my hand over her chest before carrying on, "Sam has always been here, right here. He never really left. I know he will never leave your heart. At first, I thought I was fine because he was dead, but now that he's alive, it changes everything."

She stepped back, angrily, "How can you say this? How can you leave us like this? You promised me, and you promised you weren't like Sam. You said you love Lara and me, and you still choose to leave us?" her voice started to rise.

I still know what I believed in was the right thing to do. "I will protect you, and I will find a way to change this situation so you can be a family again without someone following you. I love you and Lara so much, which is why I'm doing this. I'm not letting you go. I'm giving you to the right person you are supposed to be with. You were never mine in the first place."

She shook her head, vigorously. "No, no, no! That's not true. I'm yours. Sam left us..." she was talking, but I wasn't sure if it was to me or a statement to herself.

I stepped closer to her and brought my hand to her cheek, "Look at me, Isabel. Please."

She looked into my eyes, her tears finally spilled onto her sweet Red cheeks, "I love you both more than I can ever say. I know you might not see it now, but I'm doing the right thing. Soon you will look back and thank me for what I have done for you. God gave you Sam the second time around, don't put that to waste because you are hurt and upset with him. Remember the promises you made to him," I leaned down and picked the picture frame where she previously dropped it, "Just because he broke his promise to you, you should break yours and abandon him. He needs his girls now more than ever."

I felt my voice waver, and the knot on my throat was getting too difficult to swallow.

"No, Jack. Please don't leave us. I love you! I want *you*!" Isabel replied.

I couldn't hold any longer, so I let her go and walked towards the door without turning back as if I sealed my fate with her.

"I'll be in touch regarding our project. I wish you luck tomorrow." I felt her hand briefly land on my back, but I didn't give her time to change my mind with the gesture. I ran all the way to my car and sped off. Tears kept on falling, and I slapped the steering wheel hard every time.

I was shouting to myself, "Fuck! Fuck! Fuck!" I wailed until my car reached the beach. I jumped out of the car and ran to the sea. I didn't think about what I was doing. All I wanted was just to let out the pain I have been holding in my chest. I jumped into the water, but someone with strong arms grabbed me.

"Mr. Reed, stop." It was Alex. He pulled me out of my haze. I looked at him, and he continued, "It's just me, Sir."

I didn't respond. I just turned around and dropped my ass on the sand, bringing my knees up and resting my head on them. I felt Alex behind me sitting on the sand, too, without a word.

"You can go, Alex. I'll be fine," I said without lifting my head.

"Well, I quite enjoy a late-night sea breeze, sir," he said, sounding relaxed, at ease contrary to what I was feeling at the moment.

I know Alex for several years now, and all those years, he always seems to be calm like nothing affects him. Here I am with dried tears on my face, feeling like my world has crumbled right in front of me. I asked him, "Alex, how can be so calm all the time? You must have a great life."

He chuckled a little, "My life isn't what it seems to be."

I looked back at him. "I don't have any family or a woman who loves me," Alex said.

I turned back to look at the tall waves. "Well, I don't know what is better."

"What do you mean?" he asked.

"I have a family that loves me, a woman that loves me but not with her whole heart. I feel alone. I don't know if that is better than not having anyone around," I said.

Isabel's face keeps coming to my mind. Her beautiful golden eyes are shining through.

"Well, I would take that any day over not having anyone to love me even a bit," he said very matter of fact.

I looked at him again and saw sadness on his face — something I have never seen before.

"I know some people hide their pain better than others, but don't we all carry some sort of pain? There's no such thing as *a painless life*."

I nodded at his statement. But I had to think that this was the right thing for Isabel and her happiness is more important. "I had to give her up," I said. I don't know why I told him that, but I thought I just needed to let it out.

"Why? Because she doesn't love you with her whole heart?" Alex reiterated.

"No, because she never belonged to me and will never be mine. She and her daughter should be with her husband," I said quietly.

I thought he didn't hear me because he was quiet for a long while, but then he broke the silence, "Did she tell you that?"

"She doesn't have to. I know that is the right thing to do," I replied.

"I bet she's pissed," he said.

"What do you mean?"

"She doesn't seem to be the kind of woman who needs others to tell her what to do. But you just did that by telling her precisely that."

I didn't think of that. I blurted, "I guess you're right. But it doesn't change the fact that it's the right thing to do. I don't want to change my mind. I have to focus now on moving forward, making sure they are safe. Tomorrow, when I arrive in England, I will have a meeting with the team and take it from there. I need to give Isabel and Lara the happiness they deserve. I'm determined to make them happy, no matter what."

I stood up and went back to the car and I drove back to the villa. I gently entered the bedroom and noticed that Isabel wasn't in bed. For a moment, I was worried, so I went back to where I left her earlier. I heard her sobbing. I didn't bother her, as I have made up my mind. I turned around and went back to the bedroom to pack my things.

Just before going in for a shower, I sent Caroline a text message. She's one of the PAs I hired. I asked her to book me a flight first thing in the morning from Portugal back home. Just for myself. Everything has been arranged, but the pain in my chest was hard to bear. I just wish I could get over it quickly as I don't see how I will be able to live like this.

I only had a couple of hours of sleep. I feel like *shit*.

Before I left, I went to say goodbye to Lara. She was still asleep but woke when I dropped a kiss on her forehead.

"Good morning, Jack," Lara said groaning.

"Go back to sleep, sweet pea. I just came to say goodbye. I'm flying back home," I said to her.

She was confused, so I assured her, "I have a lot of work that needs my attention, darling, and both you and your mum still have time before school starts. So enjoy, and I will see you when you get back, all right?"

I can feel a lump on my throat. The pain in my heart was excruciating, but I know I have to appear strong. Lara shouldn't see my pain.

"Okay, will you call us every day?" she said.

I reassured her, "Of course. Now go back to sleep and look after your mother for me, okay?"

"Yes, I love you, Jack," she said as she was about to doze off.

"Love you, too, turnip."

With one last look, I left the room and took a long breath, holding my emotions in. I didn't realise I wasn't alone until I turned to the staircase. Isabel was there, too, but she looks cold with her red and puffy eyes, probably from crying all night. I wished she wan't there because it's hard to say goodbye to her.

"I see you can't get away any faster. I thought I would at least have the morning to talk to you. But you are already leaving, just like that," she said, accusing me.

"Isabel, please don't make this harder than it already is," I said, turning to the stairs and rushing down them. I was trying to get away, but she followed me on my heels.

"Don't go," she said as I have my hand on the front door.

I shook my head, and a tear escaped my eyes. I turned slowly, looking into her eyes. She saw my pain and rushed to me, hugging me close to her.

"I love you, Jack. I can't let you go," she said, breaking and bringing me with her on her pain.

"I know. But you love Sam, too. And he's your husband."

She nodded slightly but didn't let me go.

"I will always be there for you and Lara. Please don't hate me for this," I pleaded.

"I will never hate you. You are the best man I ever met. I don't know if..."

I interrupted, "Shhh. You will be happy, trust me." My heart knew this was the right thing to do, even though it hurts.

"We will talk soon. I have to go," I said, gently removing her arms binding around my neck.

"See you ba... Isabel," bidding goodbye while rushing out the door.

Alex and Pedro were waiting in the car to take me to the airport.

Isabel had a hand over her mouth in front of the porch, looking at the car as Pedro drove off. We are both in pain, but I know her pain would cease soon.

"Everything all right, Sir?" asked Alex.

"Yes. Do you have everyone in position for today's meeting?" I asked.

"Yes, Sir. As we speak, Sam is on his way home. When I come back from the airport, I will personally escort Ms. Winter to the meeting and secure her safety at all times," Alex replied.

I nodded, "I'm meeting the team in England, and I'll let you know of the outcome. Just..." the lump on my throat was not going away.

"I'll keep them safe, Sir," he said softer, who sounded not like himself at all.

I turned to gaze outside and saw this beautiful place, where a few weeks ago, the love of my life said yes to be my wife. Now, I'm going home alone, with only determination to keep them safe but away from me. I don't know how I will be able to keep them safe from such dangerous people, but I will not forgive myself if anything happens to them.

My girls... I can't even call them 'my girls' anymore. They are not mine. They are his.

CHAPTER 7

Isabel

It is official — life is a fucking joke. Just when I thought I couldn't be happier, shit happens to show me that happiness is just an illusion. Jack left us - a man who thinks he knows what we want or need. Yes, I still love Sam, but it's not the same love I feel towards Jack. He doubted my feelings. He didn't believe I wanted him because, in that stubborn head of his, he firmly believes I should be with Sam. After all, he is my husband, and he is the father of my daughter. I have to prove him wrong, don't I? I didn't let him go, not really.

This is temporary. I'm going to see Sam as I needed answers, and when I have them, I will close that chapter and start anew with Jack. I know how much he loves me. I saw his pain, the anguish on those Green eyes of his. The single tear that fell over his handsome face tore my heart even more into pieces.

I ran upstairs, got into the shower, and dressed up. I let my mum know I was going to be out, and I wasn't sure how long, so she has to spend the day with Lara. My mum loves Lara, so of course, she was more than happy to oblige.

When I heard the car at the front of our house, I opened the door determined. Alex was there with an open back door waiting for me. I was surprised he didn't go with Jack as he is his bodyguard.

"Alex? You didn't go with Jack?" I asked, wondering.

He shook his head, "I'm in charge of your safety Ms. Winter."

"Oh, please call me Isabel," I said.

When Jack asked me to marry him, he used my maiden name, Sousa, which made me love him more for that. For some reason, I didn't feel like a Winter anymore.

Alex cleared his throat and carried on, "Yes, Ms. Isabel. Paul and Kiev will be staying at the residence for your mother and Lara's protection. One of them will accompany Lara all the time wherever she goes."

It feels reassuring to have some people around. I'm less worried about the situation, but I can't help but realise that the unknown danger my family was in is palpable. I need answers, and I am hoping meeting Sam will help all questions get answered.

"Should we go? I want to get this over with," I said, getting into the car.

Once I was in the car, it was Jack's face I could remember. His smell trail triggered my emotions. I closed my eyes briefly and opened them when Alex spoke.

"He's hurting, too," he said quietly.

I thought for a moment about him — *how is he feeling now, is he sad, is he happy?*

"This won't take long," I said sternly to which I realised it might have come off too much to Alex. "I'm sorry. I didn't mean to be harsh. It's just becoming difficult."

He didn't reply but instead turned forward.

When the car came to a stop, I look at the run-down little house by the sea. It was Sam's house to which I can't believe that he would live here, like this. Sam used to take pride in everything, especially anything that concerns his image. The place doesn't seem like him.

Alex suddenly asked, "Are you ready, Ms. Isabel?"

I deeply exhaled and nodded. We got out of the car.

"Sam is on his way here from the dock. Do you want to wait inside?"

I looked at Alex and wondered, "How? The door is locked."

"There aren't any doors locked when I'm around," he replied with a smirk.

He took a small pouch from his pocket and used it to unlock the door. It only took a few seconds for him to open it. He signalled me to enter, so I did.

I looked around the house. It was so tiny, but the inside was better than the outside. I can feel that Sam's personality reflects more on the inside of his house because of its neatness. I sat comfortably on a soft chair in the living and dining room facing the front door. Alex kept himself out of sight, but I knew he was in the kitchen to get a clear view of me. I didn't know what exactly I would say to Sam, but I know I need to hear him out, Why he left us, what was so bad that he broke his promise to me, why could he not trust me with that he had to disappear suddenly.

I was getting anxious, crossing my legs, and my hands were sweaty. I didn't have to wait long as Sam unlocked the door. He didn't notice me at first. As he entered, he locked the door behind him and put his keys inside his jacket and hung up his jacket by the front door. I observed him closely as he ran his fingers through his hair and appeared to be completely exhausted. Only when he turned and lifted his head did he realise he wasn't alone. I didn't move. Instead, I looked at him up and down, to his face, his long beard and hair. He looks so different, yet his eyes were just as I remembered. His full lips, broad shoulders, but his figure is slimmer than before.

"Isabel!" he said, shockingly but looked worried at the same time.

"What are you doing here? You shouldn't be here. Where is Jack?" he looked around and proceeded to check around the house. He stumbled upon Alex who was in the kitchen and froze.

"Who are you?" Sam said.

"Don't worry, Mr. Winter. I'm here to protect Isabel," Alex said calmly.

Sam wiped his head towards me. "I knew I shouldn't have trusted that *asshole*," he said, looking at me.

"Who are you referring to? My fiance? The man who put both Lara and me first? Who trusts me with everything? The man who has the guts to tell what my husband has not?" I said with a bitter tone.

He stood there frozen, looking into my eyes with pain. But I didn't feel sorry for him because the pain he's feeling now is nothing compared to the pain he put me through.

"Isabel, you need to leave now!" he stressed out. He turned to Alex and added, "Do your job and take her away as far from me as you can."

"Why?!" I asked.

"Because you are in danger when are you are with me."

"No, I meant, why did you leave us? I know we are in danger, but why?" I asked him, standing from where I was crossing my arms.

Sam covered his face with both his hands and moved closer to the front door. At first, I thought he was going to leave, but then he turned towards me again and rested his back on the wall beside the front door.

"I can't tell you. It will just put you and Lara more in danger," he insisted.

"Stop dodging my questions and tell me why," I was starting to get fed up with his attitude.

He crossed his arms and seemed as if he was going to confess, "Because I refused to throw the game."

"What do you mean? I don't understand," I asked, sitting back down to my chair.

Sam closed his eyes briefly and started talking, "I had been receiving threats for a while, as you might know. I was getting to the point in my career where I could say it was something I have dreamed about. A lot of publicity and money were generated both legally and... illegally. There is this group that I didn't at that time know, who made money from illegal betting. Seeing that I was the world's favourite, if I would lose the semi-finals in Spain, they would gain millions, if not billions, in bets. The day of the game came, and I received a phone call from them," I stopped him right there.

"Wait a minute. I thought you were involved with the mafia. But you are referring to these people as a group," I asked, trying to connect the dots.

"Isabel, I'm using a better term than the mafia. But you can put it that way," he said, looking at his feet.

"Go on. Don't spare any detail," I replied.

"The head of the British Mafia contacted me personally and said that if I didn't throw the game away, my wife and daughter were as good as dead. I didn't know what to do, and I was torn between doing what I'm good at or gamble your lives and I do what I always wanted to do. Charles told me that losing intentionally might throw my image away, and it will take years for me to recover from that. He came up with a plan. At first, I was a bit skeptical, and I was afraid for both of you, but Charles had contacts he could keep you and Lara safe. Before I played, he told me everything and showed me that you were both safe, so I went along with his plans."

I was gob-smacked. I couldn't believe what he was saying. I rested my head on my hand, trying to think. "Why did you not call me? Why did you not just talk to me and we could have figured this out together? I would disappear with you and Lara, and I would give up anything just to be with you, Sam. I have given up everything just to be with you before. How can you think I wouldn't do the same?"

"Isabel, you have to understand. That would mean we would have to look over our shoulders all the time. Move around from country to country. What kind of life would that be for Lara?"

"One where she had a father!" I shouted. "One where she had both her parents, where I had a husband," I continued and walked towards him. "You had no right to make such a decision on your own about how we control our lives. I can't even look at you right now!"

"You think it was easy?" Sam said.

I countered, "Easy? Easy? No. I don't think it was easy, Sam, but deciding on your own was wrong. We promised each other not to make this family fall apart, and you broke that promise. You made both Lara, and I suffer more than you ever possibly know."

"I know! I know how much you have both suffered, but you are both happier now. I know you feel I made the wrong decision, but at that time, it felt right. Now you have a man who can protect and take care of you."

"I don't see it that way, Sam. You lost your right when you decided our future for us. I came here because I wanted to hear it from you that you didn't believe in us to fight together," I said.

He shook his head. I looked him in the eye — they were full of tears which started to fall fast. "It was the right thing to do. If I lost the game, I could never give you the life you deserved!" He was shouting, and his face was starting to come close to mine.

"We wouldn't care about the money. I never cared about the money. I thought you knew me, Sam. Yet again, I'm disappointed that you don't know me after all. As long as I had you and Lara, I was happy."

"I know you, Isabel. I know that you don't care about the money and having a lavish lifestyle, but I couldn't bear thinking that I couldn't provide them to you. You were always better than me that you put my needs before yours. How could I force you to live on the run and always struggling?" Sam said.

"You made us struggle, Sam. We are struggling now, not for the money but far worst. We feel pain with loss. For what, Sam? Tell me for what?" I looked around, opening my arms. "For this?"

"No, for your happiness. For Lara's bright future as an artist. For your chance to have a family you always deserved," Sam said.

"We would have that, Sam. I love... I loved you. I was happy. Lara would have a chance as an artist regardless. I would have had a job, and with the connections I have, nothing would be different if you just believed in us instead of just yourself," I told him, trying to convince him.

Sam leaned his forehead into mine and put his hand on my cheek, "I have done what I thought was right. I wanted you both safe, which you are now. Why can you not see that?"

"I see it, Sam. I see it. But it doesn't change the fact that what you did was wrong. If you lost that game, Lara and I would still be both by your side, out of danger, and having a good life together," I cleared his tears away gently.

He looked into my eyes. Here he was, my husband, an inch away from my lips. My love for him was still there, I admit. But I'm also hurt. Suddenly, I become reminded of Jack's belief; he knew that I love Sam and that I still belong to him.

Before I could finish my thoughts, I felt Sam's warm lips against my wet lips gently touched. I kissed him back slowly, wafting his familiar scent. It seemed like an eternity has passed, and my feelings were all over the place.

I pushed off Sam's arms gently.

"I'm sorry. I'm so sorry," Sam said, taking a small step away from me. "What now?" he asked.

"Now? I don't know. I need time to think this through. Jack is helping me figure this out. What will I tell Lara?" I replied and asked.

"Nothing. You say nothing to Lara. She's too young to understand the mess I'm in," Sam said.

To which I immediately refuted, "Yes, and hiding the truth about her father is the right thing to do?" I turned my back against him.

He closes his eyes briefly and let out a sigh. He shakes his head.

"I don't know when I will tell her about this, but I *will* tell her. She deserves to know her father is alive but that's when I have figured everything out. I need to make sure we are all safe first. I need to put this right before I tell her about you," I said, but he didn't reply. He nodded and gave me a sad look, which break my heart. The man I used to know who looked so handsome now looks like not himself.

"You need a haircut and a good shave," I said before grabbing my handbag on the chair.

He chuckled a little, "What? You don't like my rugged look?"

"No," I said simply.

His smile faded, and he immediately swallowed that lump in his throat.

"This isn't the man I have fallen in love with. You better clean up as we have a lot to get through still." I didn't know what I meant by it, but I thought I needed him to start getting back to his former self. I know Jack was going to ensure Sam was protected and that he doesn't need to live like this.

"I will send some money, a new mobile phone, and some other provisions. In the meantime, if you need anything, let your *detail* know, and he will get anything for you."

"My *detail*?" he asked.

"Yes, Jack has arranged a bodyguard for you and sur-veillance around the clock for additional protection. I suggest you listen to your detail. He knows what he's doing. I will get in touch with you soon," I said, feeling my heart restricted. I thought this would be easier, somehow, but I was wrong. Seeing him, listening to him about his pain, his anguish, and kissing him, it was all too much to process. I need time and space to clear my head.

"Isabel?" I had my hand on the doorknob when his hand grabbed my shoulder. I turned slightly facing him.

"I am sorry for the pain I caused. I wanted to keep you safe. I can see where I have gone wrong, but I know there is still time." I knew what he meant, and part of me wanted so badly to get back with him for all the years we have missed. But there is also part of me that convinced me I love Jack, too. I was completely confused.

"I'll see you later, Sam," I whispered as I turned the knob and walked out the door with Alex following me.

Alex opened the car and allowed me to settle in. When he got inside, I finally broke the silence, "Are you going to call Jack?" My voice was so weak I almost didn't recognise it as my own.

"Once his flight lands he will call me," he said without looking my way.

Jack will know Sam, and I kissed and will assume something. I didn't realise I was crying until Alex spoke again.

"Ms. Isabel, are you okay?" I touched my cheek, where my tears were rolling down.

"No," I didn't want to elaborate, so I turned to the window, thinking of everything I learned from Sam and sorting my feelings.

I was swimming for about one hour now. Everyone kept away, sensing something significant was going on. Even Lizzy just came to check on me once and realised I needed to be alone for a while. As I came out for air at the end of another lap, Alex cleared his throat, and I looked up at his very tall figure.

"What is it Alex?"

"My apologies but I was asked to pass on a message." He said, looking a little sheepish.

"Go on," I said, knowing well it would be from Jack.

"Jack has asked if you could return home as soon as possible. He found out something important."

"If it's that important for me to return, why did he not ask me himself?" *Shit,* I don't know what to feel whether I should be happy because he wants me to come home, or be sad that he didn't ask me personally, that he had to ask Alex to tell me instead.

"I'm sorry, Isabel but I was asked to pass the message to you."

"Please don't apologise. I'm the one who should be sorry for talking the way I did," I let out a heavy sigh and got out of the swimming pool.

"I call him in a little while. Thank you, Alex."

"Will you need anything else aside from the list you gave me to get Mr. Winter's provisions?"

"No, just make sure... he is safe, will you?"

"Sure," Alex said and left me once again with my own thoughts. Part of me was elated that Jack wants me back home but the other part is disappointed that it's most likely because of the danger Lara and I both are in. I never felt as lost as I think I am at this very moment. Not even when I got the news that Sam was on a plane crash and declared dead. Though I now know, he is alive, but my heart and soul are completely lost. I was sure Jack made a mistake telling me I should be with my husband, but now after speaking to Sam, after that kiss, I don't know who I am anymore. I should know what I want, right? So why was I so lost? Jack's eyes are seared in my brain while the memories of a life with Sam are playing over and over in my head.

"So are you ready to talk now 'cause I can't wait any longer," I turned to find Lizzy, leaning by the sliding doors with a cocktail glass on the one hand, and a Nata pastry on the other.

I looked down and realised I was half-emerged in the water. I got out and took the towel drying myself before speaking.

"No but I have to talk to someone at some point so why not get over with it," I mumbled. I couldn't look at Lizzy for a little while.

"Come inside. Your mum is having dinner at your uncle's house with Lara, so we are alone. Well, we're not alone, actually. We have a few fit as shit men around, but for some reason, I can't see any of them," she said looking around.

I chuckled a little and wrapped a towel around myself, "Yeah, they are quite something." I agreed while sitting on the lounge sofa.

"Okay so where did Jack go?" I looked at her, and she might have seen the pain in my face because she didn't push and instead waited to give me time to respond. I shifted my legs on the sofa and tucked them under myself.

"He has gone back home. He left us," I whispered. Lizzy just nodded waiting for me to elaborate.

"He left us, Lizzy. What else do you want to know?"

"For starters, I don't believe he left without a good reason."

"Well he did," I said, which I almost growl.

"Come on, Isabel. What happened?" I got up and started to pace the living room.

"Jack believes that I belong with Sam. He said Lara and I were never his."

Lizzy had her mouth open, staring at me. "No, he didn't say that!"

"Yes, he did. First, I thought he was an asshole for leaving me and that he was wrong. I love him, and he is the right man for me, you know? But then I spoke to Sam. Yeah, I saw him a couple of hours ago, and we talked, he explained. Don't look at me like that, Lizzy. I think he was wrong to disappear, and he made the wrong decisions, but… you know, I truly thought the love I felt for him was nothing compared to what I felt for Jack. But now that I saw him, spoke to him, kissed him…"

"You what?" Lizzy stood up and almost shouted.

"He kissed me, and I… kissed him back. I don't know, Lizzy. I'm so confused. I can't stop thinking about Jack, and now Sam.

We both sit back down, and Lizzy grabbed my hand, drawing soothing circles on my palm.

"Isabel, you know I'm here and will always be here for you no matter what the outcome is, right?"

"Yes." I whispered back.

"But I need to be honest with you. I think what Sam did was completely unforgivable. I was there when you were broken and when you struggled every night when Lara started to question you about her dad. A man who truly loves his family would never put them through that."

"I know. I feel the same, but my heart is not letting him go. I have never felt so lost." Tears were starting to fall down my face, and Lizzy hugged me tightly.

"I know, babe, and you are such an amazing person. Your heart is so pure, but you need to take a step back and clear your head only then you can make the right decision for you. Never forget, you are in control, and you don't have to choose now."

"I'm scared I will lose them."

Lizzy smiled gently, "No, you won't, honey. They both love you, but if you lose one, it means that he wasn't the right one."

"Jack left," I said weakly.

"No, he didn't. Not really. When you make a decision and if it's going to be him, believe me, he will grab you and never let go. I think he did the right thing."

"What do you mean?"

"He knows you need time to sort this mess, maybe not consciously, but deep down, he knows you need time, and he gave it to you."

I thought about that for a moment, and she did have a point. Jack is always intuitive. He seems to know what people need before they realise it themselves.

"You are probably right." I got up, wiped my face, and kissed Lizzy on her cheek.

"I'm going for a shower, and then I need to call Jack. Oh, I almost forgot, I need to go back home with Lara as soon as possible. Will you be coming with us?"

Lizzy shuffled a little on her feet and seemed to be nervous, "About that."

"What is it, Lizzy?" I asked.

"Mark and I... We are not in a good place right now. I thought I need a break to clear my head, you know."

I feel bad. My beautiful, generous best friend is having issues, and I was not there for her.

"Oh, no. Sweetheart. I'm so sorry," I hugged her tightly.

"No. It's fine. It's just a small thing, and I think this time apart is going to be good for us. Please don't worry about me. I'm fine."

"How can I not worry? Your marriage is going through a tough time, and I haven't been there for you. Not only that, you have been there for me all the time, even with this issue I'm facing."

"Oh, Isabel. Don't worry about me. This is small compared to what you are going through right now."

"What happened?" I asked as I went to the sofa and sat back down.

"I don't know. He has been acting strange lately. He has been asking me lots of questions and went through my stuff. I caught him a couple of times going through my diary. Yes, *my journal.*"

"Do you think he thinks you are cheating on him or something?"

"I asked him that, and he said no. I don't know. He's getting late-night calls too, which he says it's from work. He's also staying out late sometimes. He never stayed late before, but all of a sudden, he's staying up all night at work. Strange."

"So, you think he's cheating on you?"

"I don't know what to think. His actions don't make any sense. Anyway, when I said I needed to come to Portugal because you had an accident and you would need me, he didn't want to come with me. He said strange things, too."

"What strange things?" I asked.

"He said that I was going to get myself killed if I keep on getting involved with your *shit* and that I didn't know what I was getting myself into. I don't know what he meant by that, and I already asked. But he never explains and kept on begging me not to come here."

"Oh my god! Does Mark know about Sam? Is he one of the people who were involved in the fake accident?" I got up so fast.

"Alex!" I shouted. He didn't take long as he rushed to come through.

"Yes, Mi...?"

I didn't let him finish, "Alex, can you please get Sam to write down everyone he can remember who was involved with his fake accident?"

"Yes, sure. But may I know why?" he said.

"I need to know before I tell you any further."

"Okay, I will get right on that."

"Thank you, Alex."

When Alex was leaving, Lizzy grabbed my arm gently.

"What is it, Isabel? Do you think Mark knows about Sam?"

I didn't want to believe he could be. "I don't know, Lizzy. I hope not," I said sadly.

She looked worried now, and I could see anger was underneath it, too.

"Don't worry, okay? We will sort this out. It's probably nothing, and it has nothing to do with Sam. Don't tell him anything about it okay?"

"Yeah, you're right. It will be nothing and don't worry, I won't mention it," she whispered.

I hugged my best friend, my sister, wishing all this to go away so we can laugh again. "I'm going for a shower. Are you going to be okay?" I asked before leaving.

"Of course, I will. I have what I need," she said, picking up her cocktail and taking a sip. I smiled and left. The shower took longer than usual, as I found myself lost in thought a few times. The pain in my chest would not recede, and my head throbbed, not to mention that I felt queasy.

When I was dressed in my night-wear, I picked my phone from under the covers and was a bit hesitant to initiate a chat with Jack. What if Jack was asleep? It wasn't too late, but he traveled today, and he must have been exhausted. I decided to text him first.

"Are you up?"

He didn't answer straight away, and I was starting to think he was, in fact, asleep, but my phone vibrated suddenly.

"Yes," he replied back.

What? Just yes? For some reason, it made me angry, so I called him, and he answered on the second ring.

"Hi," he said in a small voice. He sounded tired or sad. I couldn't tell which.

"Hi," I said in a soft voice. What is wrong with me? I was supposed to be angry. I thought to start firing a quip at him. Something to get a response back, and I'm suddenly short for words. He was breathing a little harder, which I can hear him, and I wondered if he, too, felt angry. Maybe he already knew about this kiss. Why did I feel happy by the thought of Jack being jealous? I was truly out of my mind.

"Did you speak to Alex?" I asked.

To which he replied, "Yes."

"Do you need me to sort the flight back?" he asked. His voice sounded choked, heavy, different that I almost didn't recognise it.

"Before we discuss the flight back, I need to ask you a few things," I said, remembering why I was calling.

"I thought as much," he responded, not at all surprised.

"Why do you want me to go back home?" There was again a heavy silence.

"Jack?" I prompt.

"Because there are new developments which are putting both you and Lara at a greater risk there."

My brain started to turn then, "Is Sam in danger, too?"

"Yes," straight up, just like Jack. Always honest about things.

"Can you do something to ensure his safety?"

"Yes, it's being done as we speak."

"What do you mean?"

"Sam is being relocated."

"Where?"

"A place where only a few people know about."

"That doesn't bring me enough comfort. Where, Jack?"

He lets out a sigh. "Isabel, can't you trust me? After everything we have been through, you still can't trust me." At this point, he was getting angry, his voice was rising.

"Jack you know I trust you with our lives. That's not the reason I need to know."

"So what is?" he suddenly asked.

"What is what?"

"The reason, Isabel. Why do you need to know where Sam is being taken?" he was shouting now.

"Jack, I need to know he's safe."

"So trust me when I say he's safe. For fuck's sake, I'm trying to keep you safe by not telling you where to find him. If you don't know where to find him, then they don't know where to find him, either."

"What do you mean by that?" I asked.

He let out another exasperated sigh. "Isabel, you are being monitored. I found out there is someone close to you who is giving out information about Sam's whereabouts."

They know Sam is alive. I got up and went downstairs in a rush. I was rushing that breading was coming down to my pants.

"Isabel, Isabel! Come down. What are you doing?"

"Alex?" I called out.

"Yes?" he came from the kitchen.

"Where are my mother and Lara?"

"They are on their way home. I just checked about five minutes ago."

"Call again," I told Alex.

"Isabel, what is happening?" asked Jack, who was now curious more than ever.

"I need to know they are safe," I said, asking for reassurance from Alex.

"Calm down, baby. They are fine," Jack tried to ease my worries over the phone.

"Don't call me *baby*!" I shouted. I felt my throat starting to close up. Lizzy came from the living room as she must have heard the commotion.

"Isabel, are you okay?" she asked.

"Yes, Lizzy. Everything's fine." Of course, she didn't believe me. She knew me too well.

"Jack, I will call you back in a bit." I didn't wait for a response and ended the call. I felt dizzy, and my stomach contracted. I felt sick.

"Ms. Isabel. They are just around the corner." Alex said from behind me.

I didn't wait, I opened the front door and rushed outside just in time to see the electric gates opening and the car was coming into view. The relief I felt at that moment was like nothing else. I let out a heavy sob. My mum was there not too long after holding me up while I picked my little girl into my arms and sobbed into her hair.

"Mummy, what's wrong? Mummy, what is it? Are you hurt?"

"Oh, baby. Oh, my baby!" I kept saying between sobs. I was so scared for my little girl that she was in danger.

"Oh filha que foi? Anda pa dentro querida," my mum said worriedly. She ushers me inside rubbing my back.

"Are you sick, mummy?" Lara asked again.

"You look pale," she said putting both her little hands on both sides of my face.

"No, baby. I'm okay now. I just missed you, that's all."

She frowned, "I won't leave you alone again, then!" Bless her; she is sweet. I hugged her again.

"Let us go to bed," I said, already climbing the stairs.

After tucking Lara in bed and waiting for her to fall asleep, I went to my bedroom and locked the door. I need to call Jack again and finish the conversation. When I panicked earlier, I shouted at him and told him not to call me *baby*. Honestly, I was angry because he left, and now here he was making it all harder by being nice using words of endearment. It was unfair of him, for sure. I called him back, and he answered on the first ring. He must have had his phone on his hand all along.

"Isabel!" he answered.

"Yes?" I whispered.

"Everything's okay?"

"Yes, it was nothing. I just panicked."

"Understandable."

I started to cry quietly after what he said.

"Did I say something wrong? I'm so sorry bab... I mean Isabel. Please don't cry. You are safe. Lara is safe, as well as your mom. Sam is safe," he whispered the very last statement.

"I know," I said between sobs. I just needed him at that moment. I needed him around me.

"I need you, Jack. Why did you leave?"

CHAPTER 8

Jack

The pain I felt was almost unbearable; just hearing her voice made me want to go back on my decision. But then the question she asked was even worse. She nailed it. Why did I leave? The pain I heard on her small broken voice tore my heart into even smaller pieces. Why the fuck did I leave? I had to remind myself that Sam was alive, and I would be doing everything I could to give Isabel back her family.

"Isabel, please don't," I said, my voice breaking slightly. Another silent sob.

"Where are you?" she asked, which thrown me a bit. I looked around my own flat. It looked so bare, so cold. I don't understand how I could have been living here before and never feel like this before meeting Isabel.

"My place," I said.

"Why?" she asked.

"Isabel, this is where I should be."

"No, you should be by my side. You should at least be at our place."

"Oh, Isabel. That was never our place," I heard her moving around, I almost saw her pacing the room.

"How can you say that? I don't understand how easy it was for you to give up. How easy was it for you to forget this last year? You asked me to marry you for fuck sake."

She was angry, and so was I. "Do you think this is easy? Is that what you think? You have no idea how I feel right now. Isabel, I'm a *fucking* mess. I haven't eaten nor showered since I left you this morning. All I think about is you and getting you *all* safe. I won't be able to sleep until you are close by, until I can see you are safe."

"So why leave? Why cause this much pain when it's unnecessary?"

"Because you will never be mine!" I shouted. I took a ragged breath. "You need to sleep. I'll arrange the flights back home and ask Caroline to email you the information tomorrow first thing. I will also arrange for the car to be transported back. You need to rest, and we can talk when you get here."

"*Where* exactly? In your office as my *boss*, at your place as a *friend,* at our place as my *fiance*?" she asked with determination.

I let out another sigh and rub my wet eyes. I didn't even realise I had tears in them. "We'll talk soon, Isabel. Now, rest, you need it."

"I need to speak to Sam again," she said.

It made me so angry, so I squeezed the phone to a point I was afraid it would break. "I'll arrange it tomorrow morning before the flight. Now go to bed, Isabel," I said, barely containing my anger.

"Jack, please..."

"Goodnight, Isabel," I didn't let her speak again because if I did, my resolve would go to shit. I clenched my mobile in my hand and let out a roar. I walked to the bar in the living room and filled a glass with whiskey, and started to drink. I had a few drinks before, so I was beginning to feel numb. It didn't take long to lose all thoughts altogether.

I woke up startled by the sound of my mobile phone.

"Hello," I said groggily without even looking at the caller ID.

"Jack, mate, you back, and you didn't tell me?" It was Ian, of course. I completely forgot to inform him of all these issues ongoing.

"Ian, how are you?" I said, lying back down on my bed, feeling dizzy from a pounding head.

"What? How am I? Is that it? Your father just called worried out of his wits about you."

"Why would he be worried?" I asked, not understanding why he was so worked up. I heard a long sigh.

"Jack, Isabel called your dad." I bolted upright so fast that I almost lost my bearings.

"What?" I said with disbelief why she would do such a thing.

"Don't go blaming her now. She was worried and thought your dad should check on you, but when he went around last night, you didn't open the door, so he called me a hundred times throughout the night. I called you a hundred times, too, but it seemed you were dead to the world."

I rubbed my eyes, which were stinging, before I replied, "I'm okay, mate. I was just tired and had a few drinks, that's all."

"A few drinks, eh? I'm sure it was more than a few. What's wrong, Jack? You know I'm here for you, right?"

"Nothing's wrong, Ian. I'm fine." There was a long silence.

"Jack, I can see why you don't want to talk about whatever is wrong, but I just need you to know that whatever it is, you can tell me. If I can help, I will help no matter what."

"I know, I know that. But as I've said, I'm fine, so don't worry, just go and spend time with Julie."

Another silent moment before Ian responded. "Call your dad. He's worried, and he hasn't slept all night."

"I will, mate. See 'ya later."

"See 'ya," Ian said. I could hear his hesitation, but I hung up before he spoke again.

I got out of bed and went to the en-suite bathroom. When I looked in the mirror, I couldn't believe the man in the mirror starring back at me. When I caught Jessica with Ian's brother, I was distraught. I thought nothing could be worst, but yeah, I was utterly wrong. This was by far the worst thing I have been through. The woman I was truly in love with was no longer mine. I would have to watch her with another man, maybe even have more children with him. How on earth would I be able to do that? How could I cope seeing her today and not embrace her, kiss her, touch her? How am I supposed to talk to her without falling apart? I have to build my walls up so she can't get in again. I will have to deal with this as I do business. Be objective about it, straight to the issue, and find a way for her and her family to be safe together.

With my resolve strengthen, I go about my morning routine with extra care to make sure my shave is well done. I then took a long hot shower to soothe my sore muscles, moisturised my face, did my hair to perfection, and added a little concealer under my eyes to hide the tiredness. I kept reassuring myself I was doing this, so I felt somewhat my usual self. But if I were honest to myself, I was making myself presentable as possible for Isabel.

Stop, Jack. She is not yours. You gave her up. Fuck, I couldn't do anything without struggling with my inner self. How would I be able to cope when she is next to me? Even when at arms' length? *Move, Jack. Just get dressed and go to work, deal with one thing at a time.*

When I got to work, Caroline was already in. I asked her in my office, "Have you booked the flights for Isabel and Lara?" I asked as I sat on my desk.

"Yes, Sir. I also arranged the transportation of Ms. Winter's car..." just hearing Isabel's married name is another stab to my already shredded heart.

"I also have the information you needed on those assets you asked." She handed me a file. This was some information I was after from a few members of the Crown. Caroline was well-trained by Isabel. She had the same efficiency, professionalism, but she wasn't Isabel. I missed Isabel's beautiful eyes, her happy, and easy-going personality.

"Thanks. When is the flight exactly?"

"Oh, this afternoon, Sir."

"What time exactly, Caroline?" I asked, feeling annoyed. Bless her as she blushed nervously. I was rude for no reason.

"A-at 3:45 pm, Sir. They arrive at Heathrow Airport at exactly 6 pm. I arranged a driver to pick them up.

"Who is the driver?" I asked.

"It's Simon, Sir."

"Can you call him and tell him to pick me up first?" she shuffled a little but nodded.

"Also, can you arrange a meeting with my security team, please? Everyone needs to be present."

"Sir, but you have a few members abroad. Are they required to attend, too?"

"Get them to be ready for a video call."

"Yes, Sir. Anything else, Sir?" Isabel used to call me 'Sir' in the beginning when we met.

"How are the new PAs doing?" I almost forgot I had employed a few new members.

"They are doing well, but I'm sure they will be wonderful once Ms. Winter comes back and trains them herself," she said with a smile. *God,* why is this difficult? Isabel wouldn't be here to train the new staff. She will be starting her own business. I will make sure Isabel goes through with that, even amid the miss mess. I still believe she can do it.

I just nodded and logged onto my laptop. Caroline got the hint and left the office. The time was dragging by, and every time I looked at my wristwatch, only minutes had passed. My head was not at work as it should have been.

There was a loud knock on the door. Without waiting for me to answer, my father came in. He sat on the chair opposite me, crossed his legs, and folded his hands on his lap without saying a word. His patience unnerved me, his quietness, his unwavering look, which I knew too well. He used it when confronting a complicated business deal.

"You don't have to look at me like I don't want to do business with you, father," I said a bit too briskly.

He didn't move an inch, waiting for me to come out with it. I stood and turned my back to him, facing the large glass windows overlooking the city.

"What do you want to know?" I finally asked him.

"Why are you back without Isabel?"

He knew exactly why because he spoke to her already, but he wants me to say it.

"You know why. Don't you?" I tried to delay it a bit longer.

"No, I don't. Because you haven't told me yet."

He was waiting for me to say it.

"Isabel and I are over."

"Oh, are you really? That's funny because Isabel didn't seem to agree with the opinion you have. She said *you* ended it. Now, I wonder why did you end a beautiful relationship with the woman you are crazy in love with. Maybe it has something to do with the increase of security you have put in place lately?"

Yes, my dad literally misses nothing. How does he know that? What else does he know?

"That's nothing. And yes, *I* ended things with Isabel. The reasons are none of your business," I said fuming.

I had my hands turned into fists inside my pockets, straining the fabric so hard it was about to rip. I hear him standing and walked slowly towards the glass. He stands beside me in the same way I do.

"Jack, I know there is something really wrong going on, and I'm starting to worry." He turned to me, and I look at him sideways.

"Whatever it is, I can help, you know that."

"No, you can't. This is... something I need to do on my own," I told him.

"Why?"

"Look, Dad, I know you want to help, but this is dangerous, and the less you know, the better."

He went quiet for a while. "If you don't tell me, I will investigate, and I will find out for myself. So why don't you just tell me what is happening and we can figure this out together."

"Don't you even try. Do you hear me? This is not what you are used to, father. This is about life and death, and I won't have someone else I love in danger. Do you understand?"

"No, I don't understand at all. Because if you or Isabel are in some kind of danger, I'll do anything in my power to make sure you are safe. The way you feel about Isabel and her little girl, I understand why you ended your relationship with her because they were in danger, but that is not enough reason to end it, son. If you trust me as you always do, we can figure this out."

"No," I said with finality. He sighed heavily and brought his hands to my shoulders, bringing me to face him directly.

"You have two choices here - the smart choice, letting me in and we can work this out together, or the bad choice, which is shutting me out, and I will get to the bottom of it, and I will still help you even if you don't want it."

Shit, he's a good businessman. He never accepts a 'no' for an answer. And this is the reason he got this company to where it is today.

"Shit," I say, hanging my head and closing my eyes.

"Tell me, son. What's wrong? Why can't we work together?"

"You better sit down for what I'm about to tell you."

We both sit on the sofa, and I told him everything - about Sam, the reason why he disappeared, why I ended my relationship with Isabel, what I knew about the Crown, I left nothing out.

When I finished, I looked at my father, and as usual, I couldn't read his face. He was in deep thought, so I let him be.

"What a bloody mess," he murmured.

I chuckled without any humour as I was thinking the same thing. "Yes, well, I did tell you this was something dangerous, didn' I?"

"You did. But I thought it would be something less messy than this. Not a bloody real-life thriller, son."

"I understand this is a lot to take in. You don't have to worry about it. I have everything under control," I said with confidence.

"I trust you do, but I haven't changed my mind. On the contrary, knowing who we are dealing with made me more determined to work with you to solve this. I have a few connections, which I believe will be invaluable to us."

"Who are they?" I asked.

"A few people who owe me a favour."

"I don't want to involve the authorities. You know, the big fish must have people inside, and we can't trust anyone. Anyway, I'm having a meeting tonight with my team. Alex will be back with Isabel later today, and everyone must attend the meeting either in person or through a video call."

"I'll be there, of course. I need to go now. I'll get in touch with my contacts, and we can discuss it at the meeting."

"Fine, Caroline will email you the details of the meeting," I said.

My father got up and was already walking towards the door when I spoke again.

"Dad?" he turned around while holding the door with one of his hands.

"Yes, son?"

"Thank you." I didn't know how to thank him. The simple words didn't sound enough, but he smiled.

"You don't have to thank me. I'm glad you told me."

He opened the door and left. I stayed on the sofa for a while, lost with my thoughts. My father didn't say much. He didn't even push with the subject of Isabel and I once I told him the reason it ended. He probably thinks I did the right thing, too. God, if that was the right thing to do, why do I feel like I'm a fool to let her go. My heart contracted harder, just the thought of not being able to be with Isabel the way I wanted, the way my whole being was missing her.

By the time Simon arrived to pick me up so we would pick Isabel and Lara from the airport, I was feeling less stressed, and I have actually been able to do some work. Now, as I sat on the limo with my back against the privacy glass between the driver and me, my nerves were coming back with such a force, my heart was beating fast, my hands were slightly sweaty, and my legs were feeling jitters. I was nervous.

The car came to a stop, and Simon draws the privacy glass down. "Sir, will you go inside and get Ms. Winter, or would you prefer for me to go?"

"You go, Simon. I need to make a few phone calls." I find myself lying a lot lately, something I never used to do.

"Sure, Mr. Reed. I'll be right back."

"Simon? It's Jack. Please." I was getting tired of asking people to call me Jack instead of Mr. Reed.

It seemed hours had passed when I spotted Simon with Isabel and Lara coming out of the front doors. The little girl skipping, and the woman beside her was once everything to me. I lost my bearings just by looking at them. My eyes felt stinging, and a choked sound came out of my throat without my permission.

Lara was the first to jump into the limo followed by Isabel. When Lara's eyes landed on mine, she shouted, "Jack!" She jumped into my open arms, and I hugged her so tight.

"Hello, sweet pea!" I choked out.

"You came," she exclaimed.

"How could I not?" I said, stroking her hair. Lara giggled. I looked at Isabel, and she was clearly surprised to see me. She seemed to be holding her breath, her mouth was slightly open, and her eyes were searching mine. We were both frozen in time until Lara broke our silence.

"Okaaaay, do you know each other, or do you want me to introduce you?" Lara said cheekily, bringing Isabel and I back to reality.

Isabel moved forward and kissed me on the cheek, taking longer than necessary, but it wasn't really long enough for me. Her scent, her soft skin, her lips on my skin, it was all too much.

"So we'll go to dinner, and then Uncle Ian and Julie will come over to watch a movie with you Lara, while your mom and I attend a meeting. Is that okay?" I asked, looking at them.

"Oh, so you won't watch the movie with me?" she asked with that puppy look of hers, which always gets her what she wants.

"No, darling, we can do that some other time, okay? This meeting is very important, and we can't miss it."

"Fine, but you have to promise we will watch a movie before school starts?"

"Deal," I said without any hesitation. I couldn't say no. These two are the most wonderful creatures I have ever known.

Isabel let out a small smile, and it was like daybreak. It brightened her face slightly and shows her true beauty. I tried to shy my eyes away from Isabel, but I found myself keep peeking at her, and seeing her staring at me back without moving her gaze away every time it catches mine.

Dinner was quiet and awkward. If looks could kill, Isabel would have killed me that night. The situation was difficult, but I continued focusing on Lara, asking her about the holidays.

"What was the best thing about these holidays, turnip?" I asked her.

"You being with us. That is definitely the best thing for me. Wouldn't you agree, mummy?" Lara looked at Isabel expectantly, while I choked on my steak.

"I agree, sweet pea. What about you, Jack?" Isabel challenged me.

"Of course. It's the same for me. Being with both of you was the best thing I could ask for," I said, looking straight at Isabel.

"Could have fooled me," she whispered, looking at her plate.

This angered me. How could she think otherwise? I love them. These holidays were the best I ever had because I got to spend it with them. The two people I would die right now just to make sure they would be okay.

Isabel must have seen my feelings across my face when she picked a look at me. Her eyes suddenly softened, and she got slightly teary because she closed them briefly.

"Okay, what's going on? You obviously had a fight because you are now barely talking to each other. I can't stand this anymore," Lara raised her voice slightly, making both Isabel and I look her way.

"Lara, pumpkin. Everything's fine. Your mother and I. . ."

"Stop, just stop, Jack. I'm not a small child anymore. I'm nine years old, but I understand what is going on between you two," she said, crossing her arms, waiting for us to speak again.

"You're right, sweet pea. Jack and I are having a few disagreements which we are dealing with. It's normal for adults to have misunderstandings once in a while. But the thing is. . ." Isabel paused and looked into my eyes like she could read my very soul with those golden eyes of hers.

"We love each other, and there is nothing that can change that. We love *you*, and that is certainly not going to change, understand?"

Lara looked at both Isabel and I, concern showing on her sweet little face.

"Just kiss and make up, will you? I can't see Jack looking at you like he's sorry and you like. . . you want to cry mummy. Jack, just say *sorry* and mummy, forgive Jack for whatever he has done, okay?"

Isabel and I both smiled at her easy way of thinking things. If she only understood that life wasn't that easy, that the decisions made were the most difficult and the most painful ones. We both nodded at Lara, and she carried on her chirpy attitude as ever as if we hadn't had a gloom conversation moments ago.

We drop Lara at home with Ian and Julie, who were already waiting for us. I must have let my feelings emerge because I felt Isabel's hand touched my knitted brows. Without realising it, I leaned into her touch and closed my eyes. I let myself feel her soft skin brush against my eyebrows, down my cheeks, and my lips.

"Isabel, stop," I said, barely hearing my own whisper.

"Why?" she asked.

"Because this is wrong."

"Does it feel wrong? Is that why you lean into my touch?"

Persistent, I took her hand and placed it back in her lap.

"Why do you have to be so stubborn?" I asked, feeling the anger coming over me.

"I'm not stubborn. I just know what I want. *Just look at me.*"

When I looked at her, she was closer than I expected, and I took a deep breath. Her perfume came crashing into my senses, making my already weak resolve weaken a bit more. She looked at my lips, and I made myself freeze. I was barely breathing, too afraid if I moved I wouldn't be able to hold myself back.

"I can see it, Jack. In your eyes, your trembling lips. . ." her hand came to my chest pressing against it.

". . .in your racing heart. You want this as much as I do. Just let it go. Be with me right here and right now. We both want the same thing, so why keep on denying it?"

I closed my fists and closed my eyes, trying to regain my strength, reinforcing my walls. When I was about to lose myself completely, the car stopped, and our car door opened. I straightened my tie and got out so fast I was quite surprised by how quick I was. I didn't wait for Isabel. I couldn't. My legs were shaking and my hands, too. This woman will be the death of me.

CHAPTER 9

Isabel

I was so shocked at the way he got out of the car. It took me a good couple of minutes to realise I was in the car by myself, with Steve waiting while holding the car door.

My heart was beating fast; I could hear it so loud in my ears. The next feeling that came crashing was disappointment. I was utterly disappointed at how Jack ran. Yes, he ran out of the car. After seeing Sam this morning again, my mind was made up. I chose Jack; Sam is still lying, I could tell. He was holding something back, and I can't be with someone who isn't honest with me. He lost me today for good.

I remembered our conversation earlier. "So, is this better?" Sam asked me. He had shaved, trimmed his hair, and dressed much more like his old self. Yes, he was as handsome as I remembered, and my heart had skipped a bit when he came closer to me.

"Yes," I said breathlessly. Sam brought his large hand to my cheek, and the feel of his warm hand brought back so many memories, so many old feelings.

"How many times I dreamed of you. Your soft skin, your eyes, your lips. . ." he grabbed my chin and kissed me hard with so much hunger. I thought I would feel better than I did.

His lips weren't Jack's. The way he kissed me was like he didn't know me, like it was the first time we were kissing. I don't remember his kisses to be like this. But the desire was there, and it was obvious. He still had a strong effect on me, and I couldn't deny it.

Sam pushed me against the front door, and I couldn't think straight. I wanted to feel the way I felt for him before, so I let myself go and followed his lead.

"Fuck, you are here," he said, between wet kisses on my neck.

I pulled his polo shirt off and pulled his body closer to me. His physique was still quite impressive. My desire was there, but it was different. I desperately clung onto the memories we shared. Sam grabbed my leg and brought me closer to him, grinding himself against my pelvis. The sensation was wonderful, but it was scary because I felt I was doing something wrong.

"We need to talk, Sam" I said, trying to think straight. Part of me wanted this, but there was something that was stopping me.

"Later," he whispered, taking my breast out of my V neck top and sucking it.

I was so glad Alex stayed outside this time. I whimpered a little at the feel of his teeth on my nipple.

Sam groaned loudly, "God, how I missed you. Nothing compares to you, Isabel. Nothing."

His statement brought back from my desire. "What do you mean?" I asked, panting.

"It means I could never find someone like you, Isabel. The way you make me feel," he said.

I heard it differently. I pushed him back and fixed myself up.

"What's wrong?" he asked, confused.

"Nothing. I think this is going too fast," I said, trying to compose myself. I wasn't supposed to be jealous. I was engaged to another man, after all. How could I expect Sam to have spent these years without having women around? He was always flirtatious with other women. Of course, he would have fucked them when he thought he couldn't have me. This hurt me more than I thought it would.

"Five years is a long time, Sam. Do you have anyone in your life right now?"

Sam looked at me and understood what I meant. I saw something passing through his eyes, but it was brief.

"No, no one," he said without looking at me, grabbing his polo shirt from the floor and putting it back on.

I could see he was lying. "Sam, stop lying."

He didn't answer. "What is her name?" I asked, trying to hold back my anger.

"There's no one, Isabel," he said, looking annoyed.

I could sense he was hiding it for a reason, and I wanted to know what that reason was.

"Sam, I'm tired of your lies. Tell me her name. Why are you hiding it from me?"

He turned his back to me and went to the kitchen. I followed him, not letting it go. He made coffee for both of us, and I waited for his reply.

"I was in a relationship with a woman in Venezuela for about eight months. I decided to leave, and it ended." He was still not looking at me, and I knew there was more, but I had enough. How can I be with someone who is still hiding important things from me?

I got up, washed my cup, and turned to him. "I want you to know I made my decision. I can see now that this thing between us won't work. . ."

"No! Stop, Isabel. *This can work*. Don't say that," he said, standing and grabbing my hands.

"Our marriage can be fixed. We can work this out. I know we can," he said, looking into my eyes.

I wanted to believe him, but I knew I couldn't be with him after all that has happened, after what he has kept me from. I need someone who is completely honest with me. Sam isn't it. I shook my head and took my hands away from his.

"No, Sam. I can't be with you because of what you have put our daughter and me through. It's unforgivable. You are also keeping things from me even until now. You are not the man I need." I said.

"You need Jack, is that it? Is that what you are saying?!" he shouted.

"Yes! Don't you dare shout at me! I'm not the woman you once knew. A lot has changed. I'm not the wife who will follow you to the end of the earth and put her dreams on hold because of you. I'm my own person now!" I screamed back at him.

"What are you saying? Are you saying I made you give up on your dreams for me?" he asked hurt.

"No, Sam. You didn't make me do that. I chose to give up everything for you, but you never noticed that. You always saw what you wanted, not what *I wanted*. I need someone who puts Lara and me first. Someone who makes our dreams come true and that someone is Jack."

Sam was now fuming, grabbing his hair and looking at me with so much anger. "I gave up my life for you and our little girl, and you are telling me now that I don't put you first?," he said, shouting.

"You left us! You didn't put us first. You put yourself first," I shouted back.

The front door opened, and Alex was there looking so intimidating. "Is everything okay, Isabel?" Alex asked, looking at Sam straight in the eye.

I took a breath and ran my hands through my hair.

"Yes, Alex. We are done here," I said, looking at Sam. "Goodbye, Sam. I'll do my best to sort this situation out for you, and I will speak to Lara once everything has been settled. I want you to be part of her life, but that will be her decision, not mine or yours. Do you understand?" I said sternly.

"Isabel, don't go like this. We need to talk about this."

"There is nothing else to talk about. It's over," I said and left his little house feeling relieved.

When I was inside the car, I felt so light. It was like a huge weight I carried was taken off from my shoulders, and a smile came to my lips. I was now ready for my new life to start. . . with Jack. I only wished it was that easy. It's going to be a huge challenge, but I won't give up.

I got out of the car and lifted my chin up. This was just a setback that I must face, that's all. I would get him in the end. I put a smile on my face and went into Reeds Recordings building, where we were to meet with the security team. Well, 'security team' was an understatement. It was more of like a bloody army squad.

When I came into the room, everyone except Jack stood up. "Isabel, let me introduce everyone." Alex introduced me to everyone, including a few members who were on the TV screen. I knew one of the guys as he was in charge of keeping Sam safe.

"So why did I have to come back in such a rush?" I asked, looking at Jack for answers. He was still clearly shaken because he couldn't meet my eyes.

"As I mentioned to you on the phone yesterday, someone close to you is giving out information." I had a suspicion, but I was too afraid even to speak out loud.

"Let me guess, you know who it is?" I said.

Jack just nodded, and I saw a tick on his jaw. I waited for him to tell me who it was, but he was finding it hard to tell me so I spoke instead. "It's Mark, isn't it?"

Jack looked surprised. I felt my eyes sting and my throat closing.

I nodded, trying not to cry. "He probably had to. They must have something over him because he would never do anything to hurt us."

"He has been meeting a lot with a group at the Uni campus. There is more. . . he seems to be quite close to William Hamilton, and we think William is part of the Crown."

"What? Don't be ridiculous. They spend time together because they are good friends. William is not a mafia goon. He's kind and sweet. There's no way he can be working for the mafia," I said.

I saw Jack's jaw works at that. "Even snakes can be sweet, Isabel, until they bite," he said, looking straight into my eyes.

I saw it - the jealousy in his dark green eyes. That's the colour they take; they become dark green when he becomes extremely jealous. So dark that they look almost Black at times.

"He can't be," I was trying to think about anything that showed me otherwise. All our dates and conversations, William was always so attentive, sweet, and genuine, there was no way he could be a traitor or a mafia goon.

"Jack isn't saying William is mafia, but he is a person of interest. We are closely investigating him. His past is hard to track, for some reason. It's difficult to find his school, college records, and a lot more. We have everything from the University up-to-date, but before that, we can't find anything," one of Jack's people said.

"Surely, there must be some kind of mistake. Perhaps, he changed his name along the way. . ." I said, reasoning out.

"That's what we thought initially, but no. He comes from a very wealthy and powerful family. He wouldn't have been able to change his name at any stage. It's been hidden, but we will find it, I can assure you, Isabel," Jack assured.

Mr. Reed, Jack's dad, suddenly came in. "Sorry, everyone. I had a meeting which took a little longer than expected."

"It's okay, father. Take a seat," Jack said, getting his dad a chair.

His dad saw me and gave me a kind smile.

"Okay, so I just met a contact I have who can help us with this," Mr. Reed said.

"Dad, I already said we can't get the authorities involved," Jack insisted.

"I know, son. My contact is an ex MI6 agent. An old friend of mine and to your late mother. As I said before, he owes me a favour, so I asked for his help ."

Jack was surprised and quiet, trying to think, and so was everyone else in the room.

"He already gave me something quite important."

Mr. Reed dropped a file in the middle of the table, and Alex reached for it. He flipped through it and looked at Jack with excitement on his face. "Jack, this. . . we have so much info here. We can follow real leads now."

Jack took it from Alex and looked into it as well. "So we were right about William. He's part of all of this," Jack said.

My heart stopped. "What?!" I almost shouted. Jack looked at me and handed the file to me. I took it slowly as it would burn my hand at any moment. There, on the very first page, William sat in a formal family portrait. He looked ravishing young, and there was another man who looked just like him standing beside his father. His mother was next to his father, and two beautiful young girls on William's left side are smiling.

"What is this? This is just a family portrait," I said, not understanding. But then when I took a glance at the writing underneath the photo, it says:

Hamilton family, a.k.a. Crown, are one of the oldest families in England and believed to be the English mafia. For the last one hundred years, they have been tied to the Russian mafia, so their reach in the black market has been wider than before. Samuel Hamilton, the oldest son of Sebastian Hamilton, is believed to be now the head of the Crown. Whereabouts are unknown.

William Hamilton has not yet been found to be involved with the organisation, but intel tells us that William has had several meetings with people of interest in the last 12 months.

I couldn't believe what I just read. My head was spinning as I didn't realise that the people in the room discussed until Alex called my attention.

"No, Jack. There's no other way. If you want them safe, you have to live together and do whatever you would normally do. My advice is: throw an engagement party and try to act as if nothing has changed," Alex said.

"What? An engagement party? I don't understand. What did I miss?" I asked, confused, looking between Jack and Alex.

"We are not throwing a fucking engagement party. I'll move back to Isabel's place temporarily, but we won't go through with the fake engagement," Jack said.

"Oh, fake engagement?!" I asked, getting up, looking at Jack.

I was fuming. I couldn't believe my own ears.

"I think we should leave," Alex said telling everyone out saying hushed goodbyes and ending the call.

I waited for everyone to leave, and when Alex passed by me, he winked. Wait, what? Did he just wink at me? Was he giving me a reason to spend time with Jack by suggesting that we should throw an engagement party and live together? He wanted us to be together, but Jack was pushing me away. I can see it.

"If you are going to shout at me, just do it already. I have a busy day tomorrow, and I need to get to bed," he said, annoyed.

I was going to make him squirm for what he said. I walked slowly around the conference table, coming closer to Jack. He didn't get up from his seat. He was holding onto it quite tightly.

"What's wrong, Jack? You scared of me?" I made myself sound more seductive even when I was feeling angry.

"No, why would I be?" he said, trying to sound nonchalant but failing.

I chuckled and leaned my backside against the table close to him.

"So, our engagement is fake, eh?" I splayed my hand on the table straight in front of him.

"You haven't asked for the ring back. Perhaps, it was a fake, too?" I asked.

Jack let go of his chair and folded his hands on top of the table, but was avoiding to look at me.

"Isabel, let us not play games."

"Games? You know me better than that, Jack. You know me well enough to know that I don't play games," I grabbed his chin, and without any hesitation, I kissed him, forcing his lips apart with my tongue.

He was trying to hold back, but soon, it was clear that he lost the battle as he grabbed my face and returned the heated kiss, but I pushed him away. The desire I saw on his face was what I wanted. I licked my lips and smirked back at him.

"Let us go home, baby. It's late, and you need to go to bed because tomorrow you will be extremely busy," I said playfully, getting up and walking away from him.

I was in the lift when he caught up with me. If it were up to me, I would make him come right here in the lift, but I knew him too well. He would blame himself and somehow would build his high walls even further. I wanted those walls to crumble down and not higher.

We were both quiet during the ride home, and when we entered the house, it was too quiet that my face must have shown my worry when Jack spoke.

"Don't worry; Lara is asleep. Ian and Julie are in the kitchen," Jack whispered.

I wasn't sure how Jack knew that, but he let out a soft smile that made my tummy flutter with butterflies.

"Alex texted me just before we arrived," Jack said.

Of course, Alex would do that. He oversees everyone's security that he would update Jack about Lara. I didn't say another word, and walked straight to the kitchen. I found Ian and Julie, just as Jack said, having coffee.

"Hi guys," I said, letting them know we were home.

"Oh, hi!" said Julie. I have only met Julie a few times, but I like her a lot.

"Hey, you!" said Ian coming for a hug and a kiss on my cheek.

Just as I thought he was about to pull away from the kiss, he whispered, "Just a few hours with you, and his colour has changed, eh?" He was referring to Jack, which made me smile. I shook my head slightly.

"Do you want to stay over? It's a little late," I said, looking at Julie.

"No, we'll go home. We need. . . we have to. . ." Ian was trying to say something to Julie without us knowing the real reason why they wanted to go home.

Jack kept quiet. When I looked over my shoulder, he had a distant look with a slight smirk on his lips. My heart stopped for a second, and my breath left me in a hoosh. The sound of it seemed to have brought him back to reality because he noticed it. He looked at me with his beautiful sparkling green eyes staring back at mine. That look was one I knew too well. It was his love, passion, and lust all coming through in just one look.

"Hmm. . . we are leaving. I'll call you tomorrow, mate," said Ian in a rush patting Jack's shoulder on his way out.

Jack broke the trance we were both in but left me breathless. How was I supposed to be patient when he looked at me like that? Why was he so stubborn that he couldn't see that we should be together?

"I'll stay in the guest room," he said, shattering my tattered heart.

"Really? And how will you explain that to Lara?" I said, crossing my arms.

"Isabel, I can't sleep with you," he said without looking at me, his voice shaking slightly.

"Stop being a baby. As Alex said, we have to behave as if nothing has changed between the two of us. So we will sleep together even if you find it repulsive," I said angrily, turning on my heels towards the staircase and climbing up as fast as my legs could go. I felt tears running down my face, so I locked myself in the en-suite bathroom and dropping onto my knees, feeling exhausted and sick. I had to bend over the loo to throw up.

"Isabel, are you okay? Can I come in?" Jack was trying to get in, but the door was locked.

"I'm okay. Just give me a minute," I said between heaves. God, everything I ate at dinner was all gone. I was feeling lightheaded, so I laid my head on the tiled floor, trying to get my balance again.

"Isabel, please let me in," Jack was insisting at the door.

I slowly got on my knees and opened the door. Jack came rushing in.

"Oh my god, Isabel. You are as white as a ghost," Jack said, grabbing me under my knees and picking me up. He took me to bed, laid my head on the soft pillows. He dashed to the bathroom and got a wet towel to clean my mouth.

I was feeling weak I could barely keep my eyes open. Jack went to the bathroom again returning with a wet towel, but only this time, he placed it on top of my forehead.

"I'll ask Alex to call the doctor," Jack said, taking his phone out of his pocket.

I grabbed his hand, "No, I'll be fine. I'm just tired. I'll be fine in the morning. I think I just need to sleep." I whispered at him while closing my eyes.

The last thing I remembered was Jack's lips on my forehead, where the wet towel was only moments ago. It was just what I needed.

When I woke up, I felt a stabbing pain in my tummy. I bent slightly with a moan.

"Isabel? What is it? What's wrong?" Jack's hand was on my face. He was still wearing the same suit he wore from yesterday less the tie.

"I'm fine. It's probably the tummy cramps I get every month," I said, trying to sound not worried. But I was worried because I don't know what was going on. The pain I felt was different, but I thought of keeping it to myself and not let Jack know about it, so he wouldn't worry.

He was convinced that there was nothing to worry about, so he got up and gave me a little smile.

"I'll just take a shower. Are you sure you are going to be all right?" he asked.

I nodded back as an answer. "Of course, I'll go and make breakfast."

"No, you won't. You need to rest. You still look exhausted. I can make breakfast before leaving for work," Jack replied back.

"Can I go to work today, mum?" I asked playfully.

"What work?"

Did he just ask me that?

"My job. *Your PA, Mr. Reed,*" I said, emphasising the last part.

"I thought we have talked about this in Portugal," he said, returning to me and sitting beside me on the bed.

"Yes, but things have changed."

"Didn't you say we had to behave as if nothing has changed? Well, we have discussed and agreed on this. You are opening your own business," Jack explains.

He can be very bossy, but I liked his bossiness.

"Really? So the engagement party will have to go ahead then," I challenged.

Jack let out a sigh and pinched the bridge of his nose. "Isabel, stop."

"Stop what, Jack?"

"Look, I don't have time to discuss this right now."

"Fine. I'll pick up at lunch, and we can then discuss this," I said, determined to get through to him.

Jack got up and looked completely exhausted, too. He has probably slept only a few hours.

"Fine," he said, turning and getting into the bathroom. I almost followed him, but I was still feeling light-headed and quite nauseous, too.

I was probably coming down with some tummy bug or something. I must have fallen asleep again because I haven't noticed Jack getting dressed or anything. I just felt sweet lips on my cheek so lightly, just like a feather. Then I wafted the strong smell of coffee.

"I have to go. But I made you some breakfast. If you're not well, please call the doctor. You still look sick."

"I'm just tired, that's all," I said, convincing him not to worry.

"Yes, you said that already," he said. He looked reluctant to leave me.

"You could always stay and take care of me," I said persistently.

"Alex will be checking on you."

"Of course, Alex. . ." I said, disappointed yet again.

"Sam asked to speak with you," Jack said.

I was shocked into silence.

"I'll arrange a video call for tonight," he continued.

"No," I said.

"What?" Jack asked.

"No, I'll call him when I see fit, not when he wants," I said with conviction.

Jack smiled a little but was quick enough to hide it. "As you wish." He then left.

When I took the first sip of my coffee, my stomach clenched. I had to run to the bathroom to throw up. I was on the floor again when Alex knocked on the bedroom door.

"Isabel, may I come in?" Alex asked.

I looked at myself and found I was in my nightgown. Jack must have changed my clothes. The nightgown was a long one and was decent-looking, so I answered him, "Come in, Alex."

He came in, and I was washing my mouth and face when he spoke again.

"Are you still feeling sick? Can I call you a doctor?"

"No, Alex. I'll be fine, but thank you," I said.

"Jack asked me to make sure you would see a doctor if you were sick again."

"Well, Jack isn't here, and it's not him that is being sick, so. . ." I looked at him straight in the eye.

"Okay, but if you're not feeling any better by lunchtime, I will have to call you a doctor, Isabel."

"Yes, Alex. Sure."

"Do you need anything at all?" he asked.

"Is Lara awake?"

"Yes, Jack asked her not to disturb you just before he left. We have been playing a few board games."

"Thank you, Alex. I know that's not your job. So thank you."

"Please, you don't have to thank me. Lara is wonderful. She reminds me of someone I knew a long time ago."

I was intrigued. I know nothing about Alex. I would have to learn a little about this big man who seemed to have no feelings at all. I could see that sometimes he has, and he just chose not to show them very often.

"I'll be down in a little while," I said.

Alex left the room, but I was still feeling queasy. I drank my coffee and ate a croissant but left the eggs. Just looking at them made my stomach clench.

I was thinking about Sam's situation when my alarm went off. Meaning it was time to get ready and meet Jack. Hopefully, he would see that this was ridiculous, and we should be together. Yes, I indeed have strong feelings for Sam. Of course, he's my husband, and we have shared so much in the past, but he lied and continues to lie to me today, so he's not the man for me. What he has done to both Lara and me is unforgivable, and I could never trust him again. I have a strange feeling that he's still hiding something important from me. I don't know yet what it is, but I know it's something big, and something that has to do with a woman. I believe in time, my feelings for Sam will go away. At least it will diminish a considerable amount over time. Jack has nothing to worry about it, but he's so stubborn that it will be hard to make him see the truth.

CHAPTER 10

Jack

"How is she?" I asked, worrying about Isabel. She looked so ill that I planned to stay beside her, but I needed to go through with the plan so she can't know.

"She still not well, but she hasn't thrown up since this morning," Alex said.

He called me, letting me know that Isabel has been sick as I was driving on my way to the office. I almost turned around, but he assured me that she was okay, and he would take care of her. I still felt anxious, leaving her in the care of someone else.

"Where is she?" I asked, trying to imagine her.

"She's in the courtyard with Lara. They are cutting some flowers," Alex replied. I could almost see her delicate fingers brush the flower petals and her beautiful face close to the blooms taking in their scent. Her lips stretched into a smile as the flower sent hits her senses. My heart almost sped up, just thinking of her gentleness. She makes me want to go home and spend time with her.

"Keep me updated, will you?" I asked Alex, trying to rid the thoughts about her I had earlier.

"Of course, Jack. She asked me if I could drive Lara to her friend's house while she spends her lunch with you."

"No, send Ivo and John. They stay with Lara at all times. I want you with Isabel to keep an eye out," I said firmly.

"Yes, Sir. Anything else?" Alex asked.

"No, that's all. Thank you," I ended the call feeling so exhausted. I have forgotten how to sleep without having so much to worry about. I think I have grown older in the last four weeks. But I wouldn't trade what I have now for anything else. Having Isabel and Lara around changed my life. They have shown what real love is like. I don't know what I will do without them when all of this is over, when they go back to Sam.

Stop, Jack. Stop worrying like this. Worry about one thing at a time.

A light knock at my office door paused my thoughts. My father entered, and I could see the look of concern on his face.

"How are you, son?" he asked while sitting down.

I let out a long sigh and rubbed my hands over my face. "I'm all right, I guess?" I said and continued, "I need to be here. If I'm not here working trying to keep my mind off things, I'll go crazy."

To say it was an understatement. I think I was already going crazy.

"Why are you doing this to yourself?" my dad asked. I couldn't understand what he meant, so he went on.

"I know you think you are protecting them and that if Sam's alive, your relationship with Isabel is over. But everyone, including me, feels that she doesn't think so. So I will ask you again. Why are you doing this to yourself?"

"Dad, how can I be with Isabel knowing she loves Sam still? That she. . . *they,* will never be truly mine? They are a family, and I know Isabel doesn't want to see it now because she's upset with him. But they have a long history, heck, they have a daughter. She will regret it if she stays with me. Sooner or later, she'll realise she belongs with him and not me. And before that happens, I just think it's best for everyone just to end it."

My father chuckled and felt amused. He shook his head, leaned into the desk, and clasped my hands with his. "Son, she loves you deeply. Believe that. She's the most level-headed woman I know; even your mother wasn't like that. Isabel knows what she is doing, who she wants in her life, and you are just the one making this complicated for everyone. I know, I know. . . you are going to tell me they are not yours, but they are, son. Assuming she was divorced, there would always be a part of

Sam in her heart because of Lara. Would you not be in her life only because of that? She loves *you*, not him."

I gave it a thought about a few times, but I can't make myself believe this to be true. If it's true for now and later would turn out the way I thought it to be, I would be devastated.

"I don't know what to believe anymore. I'm afraid. Afraid that Isabel might leave me when I think I have it all. I can't let that happen."

"But you have it all. You are the only one who can't see it that way. Let us sort this mess and see how things move forward, okay? Don't make any decisions that one day you'll regret," Dad said.

I wanted to lash my anger out at something. I nodded at him, not wanting to speak in case my voice cracks.

"Good. Now, you take a few days off. I'll come in for you, and everything will be covered."

"No. I just came back from holidays, and there's so much that needs my attention. I couldn't possibly take any more time off."

"Nonsense. You are the CEO, and you can do whatever the hell you want. Plus, I'm Reeds Recordings' private contractor now so you can always put me to work."

"Dad, you rarely took time off when you were the CEO of the company, and now you are telling me I need to take a vacation?" I inquired.

"Because there are more important things in life than business. Right now, you need to keep your family intact. Family and health are important so go sort your head out and then come back to do better in your job. Besides, I missed this place so much."

"You have always been here. I rarely remember you retired," I said, chuckling. He has always been here at least three days a week. I once asked why he kept spending his time here when he could always travel around the world and experience an exciting life. To which he always answers without any hesitation, "My life is exciting when I'm with the people, and in the place I love which are both here."

My phone rang, and I saw it was Caroline's line.

"Yes?"

"Ms. Winter is here to see you, Sir."

"Send her in."

"Isabel is here," I told my father while putting the receiver down, and he gave me a smile.

"As I said, she knows what she wants," he whispered.

There was a light knock on the door, and Isabel's slim frame came into view. I looked at her pale face and her small smile; she wasn't feeling well. She shouldn't be out of bed and should be seen immediately by a doctor.

"Isabel, darling, how are you?" I asked while my father hugged and kissed her head.

"Oh, you are a little hot. Are you feeling all right?" Dad said. I rushed to her side and put my hand on her forehead, and in fact, it was slightly warmer.

"You should be in bed. Did you see a doctor?" she took my hand in hers.

"It's okay. It's probably just a bug. I took some parac-etamol. It'll soon kick in," she said weakly.

"Jack, why don't you take her home and take care of her? Let us take the fort here," my father said.

I was reluctant to drop everything at the company, but I knew that my father was right. My head wasn't here at the moment, and I needed to take care of Isabel.

"Fine, but I'll be working from home. Anything that would need my urgent attention, email me," I said, looking at my father with a stern expression so he would take my note seriously.

"Let me take you home," I told Isabel.

Her eyes soften, and she leaned a little into my shoulder.

My father's words rang in my ears like beacons, reminding me of her love for me. Could I really have her? Would she stay with me? I tried not to overthink this, but her warm body was enough to distract me.

"I'll call the doctor. He must see you," I said, making the call while walking down into the garage.

Isabel was weak, I could see it. The way she leaned into me, the way her eyes drop a little, and the way she walks. When she was safe inside the car, I went around the driver's side, but before I got in, Alex stopped me and pulled me away from the vehicle. He turned his back at the car and whispered to me, "She almost fainted just as we arrived here. She made me bring her upstairs, but there was a car that was tailing us. The dash camera recorded it, and I emailed the footage to you. I believe they know something is up."

"Is Lara safe?" I immediately asked.

"Yes, I just got a confirmation from the guys. They have been followed, too, but lost them as they were going around the city. She's now home with Julie. I hope it's okay, but I called her and asked if she was free to babysit, and she said it was fine."

It was a good call made by Alex. I felt that my heart was in my mouth. I clenched my fists so hard I thought I needed to hit something.

"Drive behind me and keep me updated if you notice someone following us. Don't give a hint that you know they are following us. As we have said before, we act normal."

Alex nodded, and I went back to the car. I was glad that Isabel was asleep, but I thought she needed to know, so I woke her up gently.

"Isabel, are you okay?" I asked.

"Yes, I'm just tired. I need to sleep a little, and I think I'm going to be fine," she whispered.

She was ill, and I was worried, so I drove home as fast as I could. I was concerned for her because she would gesture that her tummy was painful and in discomfort. When we arrived home, I carried her to her bed. Lara came in, rushing to check on her mother.

"Is mummy okay, Jack?" she asked, worried.

"No, sweetheart. She's not well, but the doctor will be here shortly to check," I said, trying not to show how worried I was, so Lara wouldn't worry too much either.

Lara went to Isabel's side and kissed her cheek, waking her up.

"Oh, hi baby," Isabel said with eyes half-opened.

"Can I get you something, mummy?" Lara asked.

"No, sweet pea. I'm fine. I'm just a little bit tired," Isabel replied.

"Okay, I'll be downstairs at the piano to practice. Is that okay? Are you going to be all right?"

"Of course. I would love to hear you play. You can leave my bedroom door open so I can listen."

Lara nodded and ran downstairs. I could see she wanted to make Isabel better, and so do I, but I just didn't know what to do. I stripped off my suit jacket and loosened up my tie as well. I took off my shoes and went to lie down next to Isabel. I hugged her tightly and whispered, "Is this okay?"

"It's perfect," she whispered back.

Her soothing voice made my heart soften so much so that I forgot we had an ongoing issue between us. This was just what I wanted - she in my arms, saying this is perfect. A little later, she fell asleep again.

The moment was cut off when the doctor arrived with Alex bringing him to the room. I slowly got up, and Isabel moaned slightly, but she was still sleeping. I shook the doctor's hand and introduced myself.

"Good afternoon, Mr. Reed. How do you do?" the doctor asked.

"I'm fine, thank you. Dr. Shelly, my fiance, is not well. I'm quite worried because she has been throwing up, feeling nauseous, warmer than usual, and she appears to be weak. She said it was probably from being tired, but she hasn't been doing anything else lately."

"Okay, let me examine her and talk to her, so I know a bit more about the situation. If you don't mind waiting outside for me, I would appreciate that."

I didn't want to leave her side, but I also respected the doctor's request. "Sure," I turned and left the room, closing the door behind me softly.

I found myself pacing the corridor fidgeting with my hands. What's wrong with me? I used to be in control of everything, but anything bad happens to Isabel or Lara, I immediately lose it. I was so busy chastising myself I didn't notice Dr. Shelly came out of the room.

"Doctor! How is she?" I asked.

Doctor Shelly wasn't looking at me. The look on his face seemed to be unsure, to which he replied, "Jack, I want to run a few blood tests. There is nothing wrong with her, high temperature can indicate an infection of some sort, but I need to run a few more tests just so I can be sure of my findings."

He looked at me as if he wanted to say something but didn't bother to continue.

"What is it, Dr. Shelly? There's something that you aren't telling me." I inquired.

"I'm sorry, Jack, but I'm following the patient's request not to talk about it further. I suggest you talk to her about it after she has rested. We'll do some blood tests tomorrow, so when she feels better, kindly have her come in. In the meantime, get her these antibiotics for the infection."

I was wondering what Isabel doesn't want me to know. I may have panicked because Dr. Shelly interrupted, "Jack, please don't panic. You are just overthinking this. Maybe this is personal for her, so let us try to respect that for now. I'll see you both tomorrow."

Dr. Shelly patted my shoulder and shrugged as he left. I stood staring at the room with the prescription on my hand. I kept on wondering what it was that Isabel wouldn't want to disclose to me. I couldn't go into the room and ask her about it because she needed to rest. I took a deep breath and called Alex to go to the pharmacy and get the medication Dr. Shelly asked. I cracked the door open to check on Isabel. She was on her side, so I slowly walked over to her and sat beside her. She didn't move but I knew she was awake. I whispered to her ear, "How are you feeling?" while tracing my thumb over her bare shoulder to soothe her.

"Tired. Really tired," she whispered back. She wiped her face, and I knew she was crying. I climbed up the bed and brought her into my chest, hugging her close to me, trying to soothe her pain.

"What can I do for you, Isabel? Tell me and I will do it. I can't bear seeing you going through this pain."

She cried harder while shaking her head at the same time. I couldn't help it but cry, too. I realised she has been suffering all of this time because of me.

"Please don't cry, baby. I can't bear it any longer. I'm yours, no matter what. My heart, my soul, belongs to you, Isabel. Please don't cry." I was holding her face close to mine, willing her to see how true my words were. It was so clear to me now - I couldn't care less if she would leave me for Sam. Even for the littlest time, I can spend it with her. The memories will stay with me forever, and I will cherish them. The most important thing is right now, Isabel is with me. I kissed her as I missed her so much. It has been so long since we last kissed, but at this moment, she filled the void I had in me.

"I'm so sorry, baby. I have been so stupid. I broke my promise to you. I promised I wouldn't hurt you, and I did," I said with my voice small and vulnerable.

"Shh. . ." she pressed her hand to my cheek. "Can we go to sleep now? I'm exhausted," she said weakly.

I nodded and got up. Isabel gave me a puzzled look, but she realised what I was doing when I started to strip down to my boxers. Her eyes followed everything I was doing at the moment. My *ego* got bigger, the longer she stared. She took a glance at my crotch and gave a little gasp. I smirked a little, and she commented while blushing, "You better wipe that smirk off your face, Mister because we are going to sleep."

"I know. It doesn't change the fact that I still got it," I said cheekily while winking at her. She smiled back, and I noticed how beautiful she is when she smiles shyly. Every time I look at her, I lose myself.

She chuckled, "It's nice to know I also got it." She gave me a little wink before turning in for the night and closing her eyes.

I climbed behind her and held her close to me feeling so light, so relaxed I have forgotten how good the moment felt.

In the morning, I woke to Lara tickling my nose. She had a huge grin on her cheeky face and whispered, "So you made up as I asked?"

I chuckled a little and looked to my left, seeing Isabel still sound asleep. I whispered back, "Yes, sweet pea. We made up."

"Good! Now can I wake mummy up?" she asked eagerly.

"No, she still not well. I'll be down in a minute to cook breakfast. Just give me five minute, okay?"

She nodded and rushed out, closing the door softly. I stayed for a few more minutes just looking at Isabel - the woman whom I love so much, who I try to engrave every curve, every fleck, every little thing to memory.

After a while, I got up and went downstairs to make breakfast and take care of Lara. I had to wake Isabel up so we could also make the first appointment with Dr. Shelly. Isabel looked a little better but was still unwell. She tried to look as if she was not affected by it, but she couldn't conceal something that was apparent.

Later that morning, we arrived at the clinic, and she was called in. I went with her, but she asked me to stay, "It won't take long. I just need a minute with Dr. Shelly, okay?"

I was a bit reluctant but conceded with a nod. It made me a bit nervous not knowing what was exactly going on, but I trusted Isabel would tell me whatever it is in time.

The wait was making me so anxious that I haven't noticed I was pacing in the waiting room until the receptionist brought me a cup of tea.

"This should help you calm down. It's a tea blend my Scottish grandmother used to make for me whenever I feel anxious," she said, smiling at me.

"Thank you," I sat and drank it, trying to focus on the tea. It didn't help, though.

"Thank you, Dr. Shelly," Isabel said as she came out from the doctor's office.

"No trouble at all, my dear. Just rest, and I'll call when the results are in." Dr. Shelly said.

I stood and rushed to them, and asked Dr. Shelly without hesitation, "When will that be, Dr. Shelly?"

He smiled back at me then looked at Isabel. She nodded back slightly.

"By the end of the day, I should have the results. I'll put a rush on them, okay?"

"Great, we'll wait for your call. Thank you!" I said gleefully.

After that, we went home. I tucked Isabel in her bed and went to find Alex.

"Let us go to the study. I want to review the dash camera. Have you got the car info from the photo you took?"

"Yes," he said without elaborating further.

I sat on the desk, and Alex switched on the TV with the dash camera footage. Seeing the video, I could hardly make out the people inside.

"We can't see any of the faces," I said.

"Yes, but I know who the driver is," Alex said firmly.

I looked at him, and his expression was a bit grim and a little worried.

"Who is it?" I asked.

"It's registered to an alias I'm familiar with. His real name is Finley Brown. He was a special ops. . ." Alex said, trying to avoid looking at me.

". . . he's a skilful sniper and brutal at hand-in-hand combat. He's an assassin for hire now for various groups," he continued.

"How do you know all of this, Alex? Did my father's contacts give you this information?"

"No," he looked at me with a serious look.

"We were in the special ops together, Jack. He got dismissed from service because he killed an entire village in Afghanistan when he lashed out on them because of the villagers lied about the location of the target we meant to apprehend."

"What? How is he roaming around freely? The military should have arrested him," I said, not believe he could be walking free.

"That's what the whole team thought. But someone bailed him out of all charges. Now we know who. . . it's the Crown." Alex said.

I couldn't believe this. How powerful is the organisation to be able to do such a thing?

"*Shit,* if they are this powerful, what chances do we have, Alex?"

Alex had the same worried look on his face.

"We need to speak to my father about this. We also need to find out why they are sending an assassin after Isabel. Do they want to kill her, too?" I said as I was getting even more nervous. I never thought I could be so afraid for her and Lara's lives.

"Not necessarily, Jack. Fin has a set of skills that only a few have. Tracking and surveillance are a few of them. Fortunately, I know him because I have worked with him. I'm also equipped with the same skills so I can anticipate most of his moves. But I think, he wanted us to know that he's following us," Alex speculated.

"So what will the next move be?" I asked.

"He now knows I'm part of your security team, so he'll try and do something different to throw me off. I'll use the same method to throw him off, too, but just leave it to me. So whatever I ask you to do, do it with no questions asked, okay?"

I nodded, "Fine. In the meantime, can you call my father and let him know about the situation? Also, can you get in touch with Sam's team and keep them informed about this. Perhaps, ask Sam if he ever saw Finley?"

He nodded in agreement. Just as I was about to get up, Alex looked at me and said, "Jack, this is going to be difficult. It might not work, but I have a plan. We can get them all safe again."

I just nodded back and sat back on my chair as Alex left. I contemplated about how complicated things were and that Isabel and Lara's safety is getting harder each day. Why the hell would Sam get his family mix up in this? I hated that guy. I couldn't understand his decision to pretend not to exist at all.

He could have simply ended up his career and not make such a wrong decision. My phone suddenly rang so I picked it up.

"Hello?"

"Hi, Jack. How are things? I have been trying to get in touch with Isabel but she isn't picking up. Is everything all right?" Lizzy said.

"Hi Lizzy. Sorry about that. Isabel doesn't feel well. She has been sleeping most of the time and the remainder, throwing up."

"What? Every bloody time I leave her, she either gets hurt or sick. What's up with that?" I chuckled a little.

"So it seems. Don't worry, though, she has done some blood tests, and we'll know more today."

"I hope so. Anyway, I just wanted to let her know that I'm back in England, and I wanted to see her."

"Oh, you're back?" I thought she would stay in Portugal for a few more weeks, so to find out that only after a few days Isabel left and she returned too, made me a little suspicious.

"Yes," she let out a sigh. "I came back to sort my divorce."

I paused. I knew Mark had given information to the Crown about Isabel, but I never thought Lizzy would leave him for it.

"Jack, he betrayed not only my best friend but also me, too. How could he do that?" she complained.

I understood Lizzy's side, but I also understood Mark only wanted to keep his wife safe. "Lizzy, I would advise against deciding on that now. Take your time. Maybe take more time away from Mark, and when all this is over, then you can make your decision."

"How can you say that, Jack? Because of my husband, Isabel and Lara are in danger."

"Yes, don't you think he was doing that to protect you?" I asked Lizzy.

I heard a sob on the other end of the line. I didn't know what to say. I didn't know how to deal with Lizzy, only Isabel knew her more than anyone did.

"Lizzy, if you want to come over and stay with us, by all means, please do. Take your time before making such a huge decision, okay?"

"I would only be in the way. Both of you have so much going on. I don't want to add," she said.

"No you wouldn't. I'm sure Isabel would be happy to have you around. I'm sure of it. And perhaps, you can lend us a hand with Lara." I replied, trying to convince her.

I have people who would do that but I thought Lizzy might need this and maybe this is what is best for Isabel, too.

"Okay then. I'll come tonight at 7 pm. Would that be okay? I just need to sort some stuff first."

"Sure. We'll see you then. Bye."

This is *exactly* what Isabel needs. To have people around that she loves and cares for her. I spent the rest of the day trying to help Isabel get comfortable, making sure she was eating enough and keeping Lara busy.

CHAPTER 11

Isabel

In my whole life, I have never felt so sick and weak even with the initial prognosis Dr. Shelly has made, it didn't make sense. There is something else I can't put my finger on. I'm just hoping it's only a bug. As I sat on the chair adjacent to Dr. Shelly in his office, I looked at him but couldn't read his expression.

"How are you feeling today, Isabel?" he asked me.

"Not great. I have been sick this morning and still feel quite nauseated. Also, I have frequent stomach cramps," I answered, honestly.

Dr. Shelly rested back into his chair as if he was contemplating something, "The urine samples show what I initially thought. You are pregnant."

Tears sprung into my eyes immediately. They were tears of happiness; imagine, I'm giving my family a child, especially Jack, who has been longing for one. I know this is what he needs. I was smiling while crying when I looked at Dr. Shelly. He was, however, not smiling. He had a serious expression on his face, which I could read clearly that he wasn't happy.

"What is it, Dr. Shelly?"

"Your urine sample also showed some abnormality, which I'm not quite sure about. . ."

"But you are worried about," I finished for him.

"Yes," he said nodding.

"It could be nothing serious, but I want to make sure, so the blood tests you'll have to do in a minute will give me a bit more to go on."

"But it could be serious. What is it that you think it could be?"

"Isabel, let us take a step at a time, okay? Don't panic. Once I have the blood results, we will talk about it. For now, let us just take it easy and start to take folic acid, the antibiotics I prescribed yesterday are still okay for your situation, so keep taking those too."

He got up, "The nurse will be here in a minute for the blood tests."

"Thanks," I whispered as Dr. Shelly exited from the office by a side door. My thoughts were all jumbled up with worry and happiness, too. I was pregnant with Jack's baby! *God, how will he take the news? Should I just tell him right away? No, I need to wait for the results. But how long will that take?*

My thoughts were interrupted by the smiling nurse who came into the room.

"Hello, Isabel. How are you doing, darling?" she asked.

I smiled back. "Not so great. Morning sickness is horrible," I said, trying to be funny.

"Tell me about it. I had it from all of my three children. It can get overwhelming, but just remember, it's worth it in the end."

"Yes, it is,"I said, feeling happiness spreading a bit more in my chest. After taking the blood tests, I felt even weaker, and by the time Dr. Shelly came back into the room, I was tearing up all over again.

He smiled slightly before saying, "Your emotions are going to be more out of tune, but I don't want you to worry about the blood tests, okay?"

"When will I have the results?"

"I'll put a rush in, so later today, you should expect a call from me," I nodded gently.

Private health care is very costly, but it's better not to have to wait 7 to 15 days for test results.

"Great, can I just ask again not to mention anything to Jack, please. I just don't want him to know until I have the results, and we know for sure everything is okay."

"Of course, Isabel. You are my patient, so everything will be kept between us."

"Thank you, Dr. Shelly," I said, leaving Dr. Shelly's office.

"No trouble at all, my dear. Just rest and I'll call when the results are in," Dr. Shelly said at the door. Jack was at my side so fast I jumped a little.

"When will that be, Dr. Shelly?"

Dr. Shelly looked at me, and I nodded slightly.

"By the end of the day, I should have the results. I'll put a rush on them, okay?"

"Great. We'll wait for your call, and thank you," Jack said, embracing me before guiding me outside the building.

Jack was very attentive, both Lara and me. I could see how hard he was trying not to ask anything about the appointment with Dr. Shelly. But sometimes, I would catch his worried gaze.

I slept most of the day. After dinner, the doorbell went, and in came Alex with Lizzy on his heels. I jumped out of my chair, and she crashed into me.

"God, girl. Can't I leave you for a minute without you getting into trouble or getting ill?" she said, laughing.

"No, you can't. So you better never leave me again. No more holidays, no more days off, okay?" I said jokingly, too.

"How are you feeling?" she asked, moving a thread of hair away from my face.

"A little better."

"Geez, I don't want to think about how you were feeling before then, because let me tell you, you look like crap."

We all laughed at her funny streak.

"Isabel, your phone," Jack had it in his hand, it was ringing. I grabbed it with shaking hands.

"I'll take it in the study," I said, rushing out of the kitchen without giving them a chance to object.

"Hello?"

"Hello, Isabel. This is Dr. Shelly. How are you feeling?"

"Better, thank you."

"Good, good," his grim voice made my gut tightened.

"So now, I have had a chance to see the results of the blood tests. . . Isabel, it doesn't look good. I need to get you in as soon as you can get to the clinic. . ." he said something else, but I didn't catch that as my ears were ringing so bad.

"What is it, Dr. Shelly? Is it the baby?"

"Isabel, we need you in for a scan to determine the exact prognostic."

"Dr. Shelly, please, just tell me what you think it is. Is the baby, okay?"

"I can't tell you if the baby is okay without a scan. What I can tell you is that we found cancer cells. Without the scan, I can't tell you much."

Everything went silent. I couldn't hear any sound apart from my breathing. The big C. I always dread that word. I have lost a dear cousin to it. She fought for 20 years. Cancer after cancer until her body was too weak and wrecked to extreme treatments. And now, I have the same fate.

"Isabel? Isabel? Are you still there?"

"Yes," I whispered.

"The baby?" I asked.

"I know this is difficult, but hear me out. How fast can you come into my clinic?"

"I don't know. Maybe 20 to 30 minutes, I guess," I said, tears streaming down my face.

"Okay, good. Isabel, please tell Jack. He needs to know," he said gently.

I nodded, unable to contain the sobs any longer. The door of the study room flies open, and Jack kneels beside me. I didn't even realise I was on the floor.

"Isabel, what is it?" he asked, holding me against him. I couldn't muster the strength to stop crying, but we needed to move. I need to get to the clinic, so I just tell him that.

"I need to get to the clinic now," I said between sobs.

"Oh God, why Isabel? What did Dr. Shelly say?"

"I. . . I'm pregnant. . . and they. . . they found cancer cells," I finally managed to say. Jack holds my forearms and looks into my eyes, his frantic eyes looking into my teary ones.

"No, it can't be. He's mistaken," I looked away, and I noticed Lizzy was at the door tears coming down her face and her hand on her mouth. She rushed in and helped me up.

"It's going to be okay. It's most likely as Jack said a mistake. Let us get you to the clinic and end this," she said, swallowing hard and cleaning her tears and then my tears.

Jack was frozen into place, looking to the floor. *God, what is he thinking? I gave him probably the best and the worst news he could hear in the same sentence.*

"Jack!" Lizzy shouted.

"Yes, let us go," he said, turning and walked out from the study room sternly.

"Lizzy, I need you here with Lara."

"Okay, I'll stay with her, but just call me straight after, okay?"

"I will," I said. she hugged me tight and whispered into my ear.

"It will all be, but a mistake, you will see," How I wanted to believe her, but deep down I know my hunch is right. I nodded and went upstairs to change and get ready.

On the way to the clinic, Jack held my hand, but he kept really quiet and still. I think I never saw him like this, it scared me. But I also understood how shocked he must be feeling. I rested my head on his shoulder before speaking.

"I'm so sorry," I whispered. I felt like this was my fault. On one hand, I have this incredible gift, which I was so happy to give him, but on the other hand, I might have a grave illness. This would bring a lot of obstacles and could even affect our baby. How can I make this right?

My apology seemed to wake him from his comatose state.

"What? Isabel, what are you apologising for? There's nothing you have done wrong. Besides, this is all a misunderstanding. I'm sure of it," he said.

I looked up at him, and he closed his eyes briefly.

"Please, don't," he whispered.

"Jack, you need to know that there is a big chance that there's no mistake on this."

We stared at each others' eyes, and I saw that Jack knows I'm right, and it probably scared him as much as it did me.

"Together," he said with determination. I could see it, on his set of eyebrows, on his clenched jaw and on his hand, which was now cupping my face.

"Together," I responded back, closing my eyes and kissed his pressed lips. One lone tear touched my cheek, but it wasn't mine this time, this was Jack's.

He quickly cleaned it with his thumb and looked outside the car again. But this time, his thumb made little circles on my hand, he was less rigid more contemplative.

It pained me just by the thought of what our troubled future would bring. It seems when we move one step forward, we are two or three steps behind. *When will this nightmare end? God help us, give us strength.*

I felt drained, but I needed to be strong and deal with whatever would come next. So I collected myself and found every last shred of strength I have left on my body. The car came to a stop, and Jack got out and put a hand out to me with a small smile. I guess he found his strength somehow, too. Funny how much a human heart can take when there is love in it.

He held me close to him on our way to the clinic reception.

"Hi, I have an appointment with Dr. Shelly. My name is. . ." the lady stopped when someone interrupted.

"Isabel, please come on in. I have been waiting for you," Dr. Shelly was holding his office door open.

Okay, Isabel, let us do this. The baby will be okay, and the rest. . . we'll deal with it eventually.

Jack pulled me gently towards the door, and I followed his lead.

"Have a seat on the bed, Isabel. Please."

I did and Jack took the chair beside mine.

"Okay, so I guess you told Jack?" Dr. Shelly said. I nodded.

"She did. So what are we doing?" Jack said with his voice strong, confident, sounding like a command.

I knew this type of voice, and I call it his *business voice.*

"Well, what I'll be doing is the scan. I need to see if the baby is doing okay, and once that's done, I'll find the Tumor. Once I find it, I need to take its measurement and pass this on to my colleague, who is a specialist in this area."

"And then what?" Jack asked again.

"Then, we will talk about our options. But please, let us take one step at a time."

Both Jack and I nodded to Dr. Shelly's explanation.

"Now, Isabel. It'll have to be an internal scan. I will be using this here, and it can get a little uncomfortable, so try to relax, okay?"

"Okay," I said.

"Can you please remove the bottom part of your clothes and put this blanket to cover yourself. I'll go and get my assistant, and we shall start afterward," Dr. Shelly said while he patted on my shoulder.

I did what he asked me to do. By the time Dr. Shelly and his nurse came into the room, I was already lying down ready. Jack was holding my hand again, drawing little circles with his thumb. I smiled at his usual way of calming me. The first time I heard the sound in the machine, made me want to cry. I have heard this before. A little, rapid sound from the machine, the baby's heartbeat. I looked at Jack, and his eyes were glued on the screen where I couldn't see. His eyes were full of unshed tears, and his thumb was now still on my hand.

"Okay, so we have a strong, steady heartbeat. That's good," Dr. Shelly said while scanning.

"I will take some measurements and details, and we will be showing you the baby and tell you how far along we have come in just a minute."

Jack looked at me, and I saw it. I saw the same look I know I had on my face. Dr. Shelly came back later and turned the monitor so I could see the baby clearly.

"Say hello to your nine-week-old baby. Everything is fine with him as he has the right size and right development."

"Okay, so the baby is well. What about Isabel?" Jack inquired.

"I will be now looking to the outer sack and ovaries, uterus, basically everything that can produce Tumor cells."

After a while, Dr. Shelly froze when he looked at the monitor. I could see a little dark glob.

"Okay, so as I have imagined, Isabel has a cervical Tumor. See this darker glob here? This is the Tumor. The good news is, its size is small so we can do something about it early on. I need to get another doctor, Dr. Martin, to have an additional pair of eyes to see if this is malignant."

"But it could be benign, right?" Jack asked, hoping.

"There is a chance it could, in fact, be benign. Unfortunately, with the symptoms Isabel has, and the blood test results, there is only a slight chance that it could be benign," Dr. Shelly said, looking at me, and I knew it to be true.

"Okay, let's just do it, and then you can tell us what we can do," I said to Dr. Shelly. I just wanted to know what options I have without harming the baby.

The Colposcopy was really uncomfortable, and I felt sore after all of it. It took about 20 minutes, but he confirmed what I knew all along. I did have cancer. Dr. Martin took a small biopsy.

"Okay so, now we know for sure what we can do without harming the baby," I asked once we were sat back opposite Dr. Shelly's desk.

"We just need the results of the biopsy first, and then I can tell you what's the best treatment."

I just wanted to get on with it, but it seems I need to wait a little longer.

"Look, I know you are anxious, so I'll tell you some of the scenarios," Dr. Martin said.

I waited for him to explain. "If it's malignant, it looks like it's still in its early stage or in stage one. In this case, we would advise pregnancy termination and begin with chemotherapy treatment right away, so it gives you a greater chance to overcome this illness."

I shook my head. "No. No pregnancy termination."

Jack looked at me, surprised at my statement.

"What is the other option if it's stage one?" I asked without looking at Jack.

"Carry the pregnancy to term, but you need to know that by the time you deliver, you might be already in stage three. A stage that would need a much more aggressive form of medical treatment and your chances to fight it would be undoubtedly lower."

"The risks are too great, as your body is fragile from giving birth, it doesn't help."

"But it's possible," I said.

"Wait, just a minute," Jack interrupted.

"You're not truly thinking to carry this pregnancy knowing the risks are you?" he asked with his authoritative voice showing his unwillingness to agree.

"Look, both of you need to take your time and think about this. I'll give you some leaflets with all treatment methods, and once we have the results from the biopsy, we'll discuss it then."

"Just one question, Dr. Shelly. If I decide to carry the pregnancy and hold on the treatment, could I have the baby earlier?" I asked.

"Well, we can do a C-section when you're 37 weeks. This is the safest method for early delivery, if, of course, the pregnancy goes well. But let us just get the results first, okay?" Jack had a scowled look on his face. I knew at that point, he was upset with my decision. But I should be the one to be upset with him. How could he think I would abort our baby? There is a slim chance, which I will always save our baby first more than myself. I can always start treatment when I give birth even if the chances are less, I will fight with everything I have.

Jack held my hand on our way home but didn't say a word, and I didn't say anything, too. I was feeling more and more angry with him.

"You didn't call!" Lizzy shouted as I came into the kitchen when we got home.

"Sorry, Lizzy. It has been a tough day, and you are here so I can just tell you now."

Her eyes were scanning me from top to bottom while looking the same way at Jack as if she was waiting for answers.

"Don't look at me. I'll let her tell you everything. Excuse
me," he said, striding away from the conversation.

"What's wrong? Why is Jack upset, Isabel?" Lizzy asked.

I let out a long sigh and pinched the bridge on my nose.

"I need a Chamomile tea first, do you mind?" I said while
going to the kettle and set two teacups on the counter. Lizzy
was trying to give me time and space, but her foot was tapping
nervously. Once I had both teas ready, I went to the living room
and sat on the sofa. Lizzy sat next to me.

"Okay, just so you know, I found out I'm pregnant. But
I also have cervical cancer. Dr. Shelly is waiting for the biopsy
results, but nonetheless, it's cancer."

"Oh, Isabel," she said, holding my hand.

"It's okay, though. Dr. Shelly thinks it's in its earlier stage,
which is good. I think."

"And the baby?" Lizzy asked.

A big smile came to my face. "The baby is perfect. It's
growing well, and I just heard its first heartbeat."

Lizzy smiled back, happy for me.

"Why is Jack upset with you? Did he not want the baby? I
thought you both made up," she said, concerned.

I took a long deep breath before speaking. "Dr. Shelly said
that if I carry the pregnancy to term, it reduces my chances to
recover from cancer. If I have stage one now, by the time I give
birth, I might be in stage three, which is a much more aggressive
form of cancer."

Lizzy squeezed my hand a little harder. "Oh, God. He
wants you to terminate the pregnancy," she deduced, and I nodded back.

"Yeah, but I won't, Lizzy. There's still a chance I can carry
the pregnancy to 37 weeks and then start treatment. I know I
can do it, Lizzy. I know I can."

"Oh darling, if anyone could do such a thing, I know you
are that person. But just think about this, Isabel. Can you imagine what Jack feels right now? You, deciding this without ask-

ing what he thinks. Should you not be a consulting with him on this, too?"

I was afraid that would be exactly what she would tell me, and there it is but I have already made up my mind.

"What if it's worse than the doctors think? What if it's stage two? Have you given any thought about it?" Lizzy asked, and I was thrown off a bit.

"I haven't, no. I guess I need to read the leaflets Dr. Shelly gave me."

"You need to understand all the information you have and then talk to Jack about it. Don't let this ruin your relationship as you need each other now more than ever."

She was right, so I nodded and finished my tea before I turned in for the night. I fell asleep almost instantly. My tummy was sore that night, but I had some painkillers Dr. Shelly gave me, which were safe for pregnancy.

Some time in the middle of the night, I felt Jack lying next to me. I cuddled to his side, and he embraced me closer to him. I woke around 6 am throwing up, almost on the bedroom floor. Just got to the en-suite in time to throw up more. Jack was there straight away, holding my hair, and then getting a damp cloth to put on my forehead.

"I'm okay. I'm all right," I said when he picked me up and laid me down on the bed again.

"No, you're not. Just stop saying you're okay, because you're not okay!" he shouted at me while I was taken aback.

"Jack, stop," I replied.

He was pacing the floor, hands holding his hair, and he started weaving through them. I got up and stopped him by holding his face with both my hands.

"Look at me, Jack. Just look at me," I said, using my most stern voice.

"You're not going to do this to yourself. I'm okay. Everything is going to be all right."

"How can it be? Isabel, you're sick. You're sick, and there is nothing I can do about it."

"Jack, we're having a baby. You forget the most precious news we have. You are going to be a father," I said.

Jack took my hands away from him.

"Yes, well, sorry for not being happier, knowing that *my child* might just kill the woman I love."

I knew it, but hearing him say it hurt more than I thought.

"No, he won't kill me, Jack. I'll fight this. I know I can. Why can't you just trust me?"

Jack looked at me like he couldn't believe what I just said.

"You think you can fight this? Isabel, can you tell me how will you be able to overcome this? Dr. Shelly said your body, after having the baby, will be more fragile. Can you imagine if you're not stage one but stage two?"

Jack also had the same thoughts that Lizzy had.

"Isabel, try to be reasonable. Think. Six months is a long time to leave cancer untreated. Even I know that, and I don't have one."

I shook my head frantically, trying to reassure myself what he was saying was wrong. But deep down, I know it's true. Six months is a long time for cancer.

Jack came to stand in front of me. He held my forearms, and I looked up to him.

"This is difficult, Isabel. But you know I'm right. I won't lose you. You are everything to me, Isabel."

"Jack, I can't. I'm sorry, I just can't. Please don't ask me to give up our baby," his angry face got even worse.

"I'm asking you to choose to live for me, for Lara, for God's sake! Fuck!" he dropped his hands and turned his back to me.

"You don't see it. You are choosing a child, which is not even formed instead of Lara who is here and needs you. She is here, she needs her mother, don't you get that?" he faced me again.

"I'll be here for both you and Lara as well as the new baby. I'm not going anywhere," I said, determined to get through to him.

"I'm not this fragile little thing you see me as right now. I know I can fight this and bring our baby into this world. So you better get used to the idea of being a father because this is happening," I said, rushing out the bedroom into the en-suite and locking myself inside.

"Fuck!" I hear Jack shout on the other side of the room.

By now, I had tears running down my face, yet again, I contemplated why this is difficult. What did I do to deserve this? I was sobbing loudly now, so I turned on the shower so Jack couldn't hear it.

I spent most of the day reading on all the information Dr. Shelly had given me as well as doing my own research. I found that there are lots of women in the same situation as I am in. They even have forums where they discuss their struggles in fighting cancer, as well as their achievements in life. This gave me further hope that I could do this without having to terminate my pregnancy. Yes, there may be a few cases where women lost their lives due to the aggressive treatment, but there were also success stories out from this gloom situation.

I didn't see Jack since our argument this morning, but I knew he was in the study working because the door was shut, and sometimes, I would hear him on his phone. I wanted to talk to him, show him what I have found, but I knew he wasn't ready for this yet. He's a very stubborn man, and at the moment, he is scared of losing me, that's why he's upset at me.

"Isabel?" Alex's voice broke me from thinking deeply.

"Yes, Alex?"

"Sam is insisting on talking to you."

I forgot about this other issue, to be honest - Sam, his bloody mafia, and more. Well, I better get to it then.

"Is it okay if I can take it here on my laptop, Alex?" I asked him.

He nodded, and I took the call. Before I had the chance to say hi, Sam's frantic voice came as soon as his image came into view.

"Isabel, what the hell is going on? Are you okay?"

"Yes, why do you ask?" I asked.

"Why do I ask? You have been sick, and Jack just told me why," he said immediately.

"What do you mean Jack told you why?" For fuck's sake, why the hell would Jack tell Sam about my situation?

"Isabel, stop. You know exactly what I mean. I know you have cancer, and I know you are pregnant, too."

I let out a sigh. "Of course you know. And tell me why did Jack tell you this?"

"To knock some sense into you, of course!" Sam said.

"Look, Sam. I appreciate it, but it's none of your business. Besides, we don't know exactly where we stand with the final diagnosis so until I know more, nothing has been set to stone yet," I replied.

I think that should abate him. He looked almost as angry as Jack.

"Isabel, you keep forgetting, I know you."

"No Sam, you keep forgetting you do not know me at all, so leave it alone."

I was getting angrier and angrier with him. My tummy hurts, my head hurts, I felt nauseous, and I was on the verge of screaming. Sam closed his eyes and let out a long sigh.

"Isabel, I care too much about you, to even think of losing you."

"You already lost me," I whispered while not looking at him.

"No, I haven't. You are still here, alive, so you better stay that way. You might no longer want to be my wife, but you are still my little girl's mother, and she needs you, so think about her before making any decision," he said a little sad looking.

I rubbed my eyes and nodded.

"Is that it? Can I go now?" I asked, trying not to look at him.

"Just please promise me you'll think this through, will you?"

I didn't give him another chance to go on as I ended the call immediately. I felt drained now, and I missed spending time with my little girl. School has started as well as her rehearsals. By the time it was for me to pick her up, Jack had come out of the study, trying not to look at me as he passed on the corridor.

"Are you going to avoid me every day now?" I asked well, annoyed.

Jack stopped with a hand on the front doorknob.

"I'm going to pick Lara up from rehearsal."

"It's okay, I'll do it."

"Don't be daft. You need to lay down and rest."

"I'm pregnant, not invalid," I said again, annoyed.

Jack did something I was not expecting. He punched the wall beside the front door. I was so surprised that I jumped back.

"Not yet!" he shouted.

He became very aggressive. This was starting to scare me. I have never ever seen him like this. I turned to the stairwell and run upstairs, crying, scared that Jack was losing himself to anger. Well, I guess I could give him the decision he wants, but that would be the wrong decision, so I couldn't. The front door shut with a loud bang. What will I do to make him less angry, less scared?. A moment later a knock at my bedroom door came.

"Come on in," I said between sniffs.

"You okay?" Lizzy asked in a small voice. I shook my head instead of using my voice.

"He's very upset." She said.

"No, he's angry, not upset. Just because I don't do what he wants, that is it -- he goes off the rails? He's in the wrong, Lizzy. Not me," I said. She sits next to me on the bed and patted my knee.

"He doesn't know how to cope with this situation, Isabel. You need to give him a break, he's in an impossible position. On one hand, his dream is to be a father, on the other hand... you are the most important thing to him. So for him to think he might lose you. . . it's really hard for both of you."

"Yes, well I'm the one who has a time bomb inside. I'm the one who has to make the final decision. Any decision I make will be the wrong one, Lizzy. This is hard for him, I know, but understand that this is even harder for me."

"I know, and he knows it. But everyone deals with things differently. Just give him time. I'll speak to him later, and I'll help you no matter what decision you make," I hugged her and cried for a little while longer.

What would I do if I didn't have Lizzy? I didn't want to tell my mum anything until the results are back, which should be in four days.

I had four days to research as much I could on other options like natural treatments, which I knew existed but not sure how to search for those, perhaps Lizzy would help me.

Lara was so happy today, and it was contagious. I laughed a lot at dinner. She was telling us about the holiday stories her friends told her and believe there, there were a few funny ones. I caught Jack staring at me a few times, and every time he realised I was looking, he averted his eyes, but he knew I was aware of him looking at me.

"Go on, brush your teeth and get ready for bed pumpkin, I will be there in just a minute," I said, getting up and starting to clean the table.

"Leave it, I'll do that. You go up with Lara," Jack said, without looking at me. He was dropping the plates on the sink, and I was so close that I stretched and kissed his cheek. He closed his eyes as I kissed his cheek.

"Thank you," I said as I left to go upstairs and help Lara getting ready for bed.

I needed to get Jack relaxed. But I don't know-how, though. He wasn't going to come to bed any time soon. After he tidied the kitchen, he closed himself off in the study again. I'm now sitting on the bed, trying to think a way to bring him out of the damn study room and spend time with me. I went to my walk-in closet and opened the first drawer where I keep my nighties. *Yes, these nighties will do.*

I took what I had in mind out and went to get ready. Even though I was tired and still felt a bit queasy, the medication Dr. Shelly gave me helped a bit. Now was the time to bring *my* Jack back.

CHAPTER 12

Jack

I felt scared beyond belief, that led me to be angry, which in turn led to violence. I was never the type of man who would lose control, well not until Isabel came into my life. She was really good to me, but she could also make me feel things I have never felt before; hence my control kept slipping. I never wanted to scare her, but she has lost her mind. How could she choose to have this baby when she knows it would cost her life? No matter who she left behind. She couldn't see it, and I didn't know how to make her see it. I thought by telling Sam, it would help, he would make her see it, but nope. She's so stubborn, and she can't see the gravity of the situation.

I was staring into the ceiling when the study door opened slowly. I expected to see Lizzy there as she didn't leave long ago, but I certainly didn't expect Isabel to be there dressed only in a see-through burgundy one-piece. Even though I was angry at her, I couldn't help looking at her, and stop the desire to arise within me instantly.

"If you don't come to me, *I will come to you*," she said, stretching her arms up along the door frame, inclining her hip to one side and opening her legs a bit more.

I cleared my throat and moved a little on my chair before speaking.

"Isabel, I'm a little busy at the moment, but you go to bed ahead. I'll try not to stay up late."

Her face fell a little, but she soon recovered and entered the study in a slow, sexy manner that was *hot* as hell. She reached my desk and put both hands on it, jolting her perfect, full breasts closer to my face. I was holding on barely able to keep my hands where they are.

"Alex and the team are around. You shouldn't walk around the house like that, Isabel," I said, trying to sound serious but was failing big time.

The raging desire I was feeling getting out of control, and the only thing I could see was her beautiful, sexy form in front of me, ready to be taken.

"Well, if you weren't so stubborn and came to bed, I wouldn't have to walk around the house like this," she said, coming even closer to my ear, her breath, ticking my neck, making me shiver a little.

"But you know, this is kind of exciting, knowing someone could see us. . ." she whispered.

That was all it took. I grabbed her by the waist, brought her over the desk, and make her sit on my lap. She gasped, surprised by my strength and ease of what I did to her. To be honest, I was surprised myself.

"Is this what you want?" I asked her before capturing her mouth with my own to which she moaned.

This made me want to take her even more, but then I remembered she's sick and I can't do it.

"*Shit,* we can't do this," I said, grabbing her by the hair gently.

"What?" she said, confused.

"It'll be painful for you. We can't," I said, out of breath.

I felt my blood gushing all to the same place in my body.

"Of course we can. It wouldn't hurt me, I promise," she started kissing me, and I almost lost myself, but I was reminded again of her situation, so I held back.

"I have been reading about it. You don't have to worry about it. I'm not in pain, I've been taking the painkillers. I'm good, I promise. Now can you just fuck me or will I. . ." I didn't let her finish as I captured her mouth again. This time I didn't hold back. I trusted that she would tell me if she was in pain.

I ripped the flimsy one-piece she was wearing and laid her back on the desk. I opened my jeans while Isabel was opening my shirt buttons. We had a fast pace, as we both needed and craved for this. I brought my mouth to her vagina and started to French kiss it. She moaned and riddled under me, moving her pelvis with my mouth following. I slowly kissed upwards until I reached her nipples and started to suck them. She moaned a little louder as I enter her in one swift jerk.

God, she feels so good. How can I ever lose her? I rammed into her real hard with each thrust we both moan. We worked up so fast, maybe because we haven't done it in a while.

"Yes. . . Hmm. . . Yes. . ." Isabel was so close, so I moved my finger from her breast to her clit and moved it in a circular motion as I increased my tempo, just the way she liked it, and as I predicted, she came. She scratched my back as she arched her back. I wanted this feeling to carry on forever, but I couldn't hold myself. Her moans and her inner walls were tightening, so I came. We were heaving, and I was holding her close to me, breathing her sweet scent in, it was perfect.

"Now, can we go to bed?" she said with a smile on her voice.

It made me smile, too. How could I feel angry with this woman?

"Yes, we can," I whispered. "But I think you better dress my shirt, just in case somebody sees you," I suggested as she laughed at it.

With the noise we made, I doubted someone would miss what we were doing. Seeing Isabel in my shirt and a smile on her beautiful flushed face made my heart clenched.

God, how will I support her when I might lose her because of her decision.

"If you don't stop staring at me, I might really blush," she said, trying to make a joke.

"Let us get you into bed, you need to rest," I said, picking her up and cradling her in my arms.

"I can walk, you know," she said into my neck, trying to tickle me and making me smile a little further.

"I know, but I need to practice as it looks like I will be a dad, soon," I whispered.

She smiled into my neck, but she didn't respond, so I asked.

"Are you in pain?"

"No, not at all," she replied.

We went to sleep that night, but I had a few nightmares. A few of the scenes involved Isabel, and even after waking up, I could still remember bits of it. I was drenched in sweat, and I can recall images in my head of Isabel, not in a good condition. She was still asleep, though, so I went for a shower. As I was halfway to the shower, I decided to go and work out in the gym instead.

"Jack, we need to talk. It's urgent," Alex met me at the bottom of the staircase.

I saw the look of his face, and I figured it wasn't good.

"Let us go to the study," I said.

I should have gone for the shower, I thought.

Alex had an anxious look and immediately talked.

"Mark has been found dead," Alex broke the news.

"Wait, what? Mark? Lizzy's husband?" I inquired.

"Yes," he confirmed with a concerned look.

I stood and started to pace the room. "Does Lizzy know?" I asked.

"No, my guys found him alive. They did everything they could, but by the time the ambulance arrived, he had already passed away."

"Lizzy will find out about this very soon. They'll call her as she's the wife. I need to tell her," I said worriedly.

"I think it is wise that she hears this from you," Alex chimed in.

As I was on my way upstairs to the guest room, a piercing cry came from the room where I was heading. I knew Lizzy found out.

I prepared myself, and I knocked on the door. As I entered the room, I saw Lizzy on her knees with a pillow to her face trying to muffle the noise from her cries. I gently knelt beside her and removed the pillow away. I hugged her ever so tightly.

"I'm sorry, Lizzy. I'm so sorry," I whispered.

"You know?" she asked while sobbing.

"I was on my way to tell you. I just found out myself. My men tried to help, but it was already too late."

She sobbed harder, "I love him. I was going to give him a chance, Jack. Why, God, why?"

Isabel must have heard her crying because she came into the room, too. "Lizzy, what happened?!"

We both turned to her, and Lizzy broke the news as well to her. "Mark's dead. I haven't told him that I've forgiven him. I haven't had the chance to tell him I love him. Now, he's gone," Lizzy sobbed.

"Shhh. . . Oh, darling. I'm so sorry," Isabel was now crying, too.

It pained me to see so much pain from them. I can't believe that Isabel's happiness has been slowly stripped away from her life. When will this end? It's always one thing after another.

I left the room and gave them space. I went to find Alex again as I want to deal with this now.

"Alex, get my father to come over. We need to end this. It's getting out of hand now," he nodded and picked his mobile phone to call. It didn't take very long for my father to come over.

"We need to communicate with them. I need to end this now and know what they want. If it's money, I'll give it to them," I told Alex and my father.

"Jack, I don't think this is just about the money anymore. You have to understand that when someone refuses to do what they demand, they want blood shed. What you're going to do might not be enough," Alex said.

"He's right, son. They have money - plenty of money. But they want to take revenge on Sam. You know this," he said.

"So, I'll give them Sam!!!" I shouted.

At this point, I was already angry, fuming mad. I will give them Sam because the alternative presented was not an option for me.

"I'll lose neither of my girls because of Sam's mistakes. Not at their expense. He got into this mess, not them."

"Just think about this first, Jack. Think this through. Isabel will never agree to this. Besides, how do you know that they won't kill all of us once we give them Sam?" Alex replied.

He had a point. But what else could I do? They have us held onto our necks.

"They killed Mark to warn us. They know Sam's alive and that we are protecting him. I'm sure of it," I said, looking at Alex.

"Yes, I believe so. But Jack, we need to find another way, and giving up Sam doesn't stop the threat to your family."

"What will then?" I asked frustrated. I just want to get this all over with. This was too much for me. There's the fucking mafia who wants to kill all the people I love. Even if they don't kill Isabel, her situation - having cancer will.

I grabbed my hair and let out a roar. I felt like a caged animal, overwhelmed with all that's happening. My father came to me and grabbed me by the shoulders.

"Look at me, son. We'll figure this out. You just need to clear your head and concentrate on finding a solution for this," he said calmly.

It helped a little, but I was too exhausted with all of this. "Even if we find a fucking solution for this, there are other life and death issues, father," I said, turning my back at him and leaning my head against the cold glass of the study window.

"Issues such as what?" my father asked, surprised by my reply.

I let out a long sigh and finally gave in, "Isabel's sick."

There was silence in the room.

"How sick?" he asked behind me.

"She has cancer," I said.

"Son. . . you know modern medicine has become very advanced. This doesn't mean we will lose her. I'm sure if you get the right doctor. . ."

"Just stop. She has a great chance to get better, but she's refusing my help," I blurted.

"What? Why?"

"She's pregnant, so she wants to carry the pregnancy to full term and get treatment afterward. But I know that it'll be too late, I know it," I said, pacing the study again.

Alex was all stiffed in the corner, but I could see the news affected him somehow as he was the one who cared for her for a while now.

"Have you seen a specialist?" my father asked.

"Dr. Shelly has been doing some tests and whatnot. We will know for sure in a few days as to the final diagnosis."

"Son, it's too early for you to assume anything. It could all be nothing. Why are you thinking the worst for her?"

"Because we both know that she's sick," I said, exhausted from everything.

My father came to me and put a hand on my shoulder.

"Jack, let us concentrate on the issue at hand. This requires immediate attention. When you have the diagnosis, concentrate on that. I have lots of people who can help. We'll get through this, okay?" he said, trying to comfort me.

"Like mum did?" I said and regretting the moment I said it because sadness suddenly crossed my father's face. It made me even ashamed for saying such a thing.

"I'm sorry, dad. I didn't mean it. I know you did everything you could for mum."

My father gave me a sad smile, "Isabel is different. She's young."

"Are you telling me you agree with her? Should she carry the pregnancy and endanger her life even further? This is ridiculous. If the mafia doesn't kill her, cancer will, and either way, I'm going to lose her!" I shouted, desperate enough of not having a solution to this problem.

My father hugged me tightly to him. This is the first time he hugged me like this. Throughout my life, the only times I was hugged by him was during my mother's funeral, and now. I wanted to cry, but anger was much stronger, so I pushed my father away.

"No, I don't need your pity! I need a solution to all of this. So tell me father, what it is. Because that's the only thing, I need from you!" I shouted again, pointing my finger at him.

"Jack, calm down. Isabel will hear you. I think she doesn't need you to lose your shit right now. You need to be strong for her. We'll find a way to keep her safe and make sure she survives. But you need to keep your head on the game. Do you hear me?!" he demanded.

I paced the study room, fuming with my hands on my hair. I was quite surprised I still had a full head of hair because of the amount of tugging I have been doing lately, I would have thought all of my hair would have been gone by now.

"Okay, Alex. Get me Sam on a video call, now." I said. He did it as I asked.

"Sam, we need to arrange a meeting with the Crown. Do these guys who have been keeping you safe before know who we need to get in touch with to arrange that?"

"Why? What's happened?" he asked, but I cut him off.

"Just. . . answer the question," I demanded.

"I think I can get the name of the guy who made his demands from me, I guess."

"Do it now," I ordered.

He frowned and shook his head, "Jack, just tell me what is going on first. I deserve that."

I became really annoyed of him, "You fucking deserve nothing. This fucked up mess you are in, that you got us all in, is all your fault so just do what I said," I said, staring down at him through the monitor.

I may have hit a nerve because he was getting flushed with anger, but he nodded before asking a phone to one of the secure details I assigned to him.

"Carl, it's me, Sam. Yes, I'm safe. Sorry, I needed to go dark. Look, I need your help right now. I need the name of the guy who made the demands. . . Yes, from the Crown," Sam said and continued, "Never mind my safety, I need it. No, I'm not going to do something stupid. . . Frances Sharp. . . right, thank you. Bye," Sam bid good bye to Carl on the phone.

"I'm sure you heard the name. Is that all you need, Sir?" Sam said in a condescending tone.

Pissed, I ended the call without acknowledging his dig. Alex was on the phone, and I assumed he heard the call, too, and is trying to find this Frances Sharp.

"Right, what do you have in mind, son?" asked my father.

"I need to arrange a meeting with this individual and try to understand what they want."

"What are you going to ask? 'Oh, hi, mate! I was just wondering what you want from my fiance?'" my father said casually.

I looked at him hard before speaking. "More or less. I'll figure it out when I'm there."

"Jack, remember I said I had a plan?" Alex said. I didn't answer, only nodded slightly.

"Well, this might just work in our favour. I think it's a great idea for the meeting, but you know, once you acknowledge the threat directly, whatever reservations they have, will no longer be there. They might just go for the kill, right?"

"Yes, I know that Alex. But how does that work in our favour?" I asked, perplexed by his statement.

"Well. . . I think the head of the Crown will most likely meet you instead, to throw you. Remember, I said Finley would try to do something that will be unpredictable. Well, this is what I think he will do. I am almost 100 percent sure he will advise the head to meet with you, and we will be waiting," he said.

"Who's going to be waiting?" I asked.

Alex looked to my father and he nodded to him back, agreeing to his unspoken question.

"MI5."

That rendered me speechless. "Wait," I looked at my father, and he smiled a little.

"Didn't I say that the government has been compromised? They have people everywhere. This means MI5, MI6, and everyone in the government could be with them on this," I said worriedly.

"Well, you see, son. I have been busy with that. Apparently, there was a special task force who has been working infiltrating the Crown, but had no success for a long time. Some of the agents who went after them are dead. Now, I once spoke to my contacts and received a call in the middle of the night a couple of weeks ago. We have been trying to get a plan going. I think this is the right time to apply that."

"You are suggesting that this is to capture the head of the Crown?" I inquired.

"If everything goes according to plan. . . more than the head himself, even the group."

I didn't understand how my father didn't mention this to me before.

"And you are just mentioning this to me now? Don't you think I should have known?" I asked, upset and disappointed that my father kept this from me.

"Jack, your father hasn't told you because I asked him not to. I needed to make sure your actions wouldn't change course. Remember, I said, do whatever I said, and no questions asked. This is it," Alex said.

I sat back down and heaped a heavy sigh.

"Okay, but I need to know what the plan is now."

"It's simple, we need to wire you. . ." Alex said without letting him finish.

"Wait, I have seen enough spy movies to know they always frisk, and you get found."

"The technology we have. . . Well, let us just say, they would not be able to find it. Also, they might not frisk you if they agree to meet in a public place," Alex suggested.

"Wait a minute, if we do this in a public place, won't the people get in the way and they might get hurt in the process," my father asked Alex.

"Not if those people around are all agents," Alex said.

"You mean, meeting in a restaurant or cafe that all the staff and customers can be agents," I asked.

"Exactly."

"What if they pick the place? If they pick the place, they will know everyone. That won't work."

"Jack's right, Alex."

"Jack, do you think you can get him to agree to meet at Hyde Park? A perfect place that will give him the impression of security where we can make sure the agents are in place, and if anything goes sideways, we have the upper hand."

"That could work," I said, thinking.

"I'll speak to the agents, and we get you in touch with them, too. You need a burner phone to speak to the agents."

"I don't want you to meet them," my father said.

"Why? I need to know with whom I'm going to be working with. What if anything goes wrong, and I don't know who I can trust?" I asked nervously.

"I'll be there next to you, and I will be working closely with the tactic unit, so you don't have to meet anyone. If they find out that you are in any way involved with MI5, you will be dead meat," Alex said.

"Fine. Get me the number for this Frances Sharp, so I can get this over with," I said.

"Jack, I need to speak to the team at MI5, and once all the details are agreed and the plan is watertight. I'll ask you to make the call, but for now, just sit tight, okay?" Alex said.

I can't believe I have to wait for this. I just want it over and done with.

"Can you please expedite this?" I asked, feeling more and more anxious.

"Jack, this is our only chance to get them, so we need to make sure our plan doesn't have any loopholes. Just give us a little more time, okay?" I nodded but felt unsure of this. I had a bad feeling about it.

I was punching badly at the gym bag when I noticed Isabel by the doorway leaning against its frame. She looked a bit better, less pale.

"I hope you're not imagining anyone I know when you're punching that bag," Isabel joked.

I chuckled. "How's Lizzy?" I asked, out of breath. Isabel shrugged her shoulders slightly and gave me a sad look.

"She's not doing so good. I got her to sleep with the help of some pills. Lara saw her crying and was really upset, too. I had to tell her," she said, her eyes watering.

I removed my boxing gloves and cleaned my face and bare chest before grabbing her hand and tugged her to me.

"I'm so sorry, Isabel. Tell me what I can do to make this all go away."

"You can't do anything. This is life. Lizzy is strong, and she will come through. She's bruised, but she is strong, She'll pull through I'm sure of it," she said, sniffling a little.

"Has Lara gone to school?" I asked.

"No, she was too upset over Mark's death so I called the school and explained that she would be taking a week off school," Isabel said while I cleaned her tears away from her cheeks.

"When will we tell her about the baby and. . . the cancer?" Isabel looked at me without answering.

"She needs to know, Isabel. What if anything goes wrong, and she finds out, she will be even more upset."

"She's too young to deal with all of this chaos, Jack. I can't tell her about my sickness just like I can't tell her about her father until the right time," I know what she meant, but I still think Lara should know. Lara is her mother's daughter, she's strong and intelligent just like her, so I know she will under-stand. But this was Isabel's decision, so I needed to support her. I kissed the tip of Isabel's sweet little nose.

"Alright."

"But the part of the baby. . ." she smiled at me and kissed me, light and sweet, making me feel butterflies in my stomach as she deepened the kiss. God, she was risking her life to give me a child. Just the thought of her risking her life was like a bucket of freezing water, putting all the flames that were grow-ing uncontrollably inside out. I pulled myself from the kiss.

"What's wrong?" she asked frowning.

"Nothing," I said, turning to put the boxing gloves away.

"Nothing? Why did you pull away?" she asked hurt.

I collected myself before speaking. "It hurts, Isabel. It hurts so bad. I don't know how to deal with this. . . with this feeling in here," I pointed to my chest, where the burning was and where my heart was on fire and tight as if someone squeezed it.

Isabel closed her beautiful golden eyes briefly.

"I'm sorry, Jack," she said in a small voice, looking right at me. She was trying to apologise to my soul, I could see it on her penetrating stare. I didn't want her apology; I just wanted her to choose to live.

"If you just terminate the pregnancy, I just know you would be better off with your health," I implored her one last time.

"Jack, please don't ask this of me. I can't kill our child," I could argue this, but I didn't. I didn't because I knew it would be useless. I turned my back to her to hide the tears that were forming. I swallowed hard, trying to get rid of the lump on my throat.

"Are you hungry?" I asked her trying to change the painful subject.

"I am. I was going to make lunch, but came to find you instead," she said.

The day went by in a somber mood. Everyone, even the security details, were quiet and sad, but Alex seemed even more affected. I never saw anything affect Alex like this.

One night in the kitchen, Alex spoke to Lizzy. He was speaking in such a manner with his soothing and gentle voice, it was totally out of his character. Lizzy was in a bad way, I never saw her like this. I couldn't see any shred of her easy, funny, cheeky streak in her now. Her tears didn't stop falling all day, she couldn't stop going on about how bad she treated him last time they spoke. How she didn't tell him how much she loved him, how she forgave him. It was heartbreaking to watch her like this.

I slowly walked away from the kitchen and went upstairs to find Isabel reading a story to Lara. I stood at the doorway looking at both of them, how much they love each other, how Isabel spoke in a soft voice while Lara paid attention to her mother like what she was saying was the most important thing she would ever hear. If anything happens to Isabel, how will this beautiful girl cope? Her mother is everything to her, she has been mother and father to Lara. *If she dies. . . stop it, Jack.*

I left them and went to take a shower, where my thoughts went over all the arrangements that have to be made for Mark's funeral. Of course, his body has to be released before we can sort all the details out, but I'll have to make a few calls to settle most of it. I know Lizzy won't be in the right state of mind to do this, and Isabel has a lot going on too, so I will gladly sort this out — it's the least I can do for Lizzy.

CHAPTER 13

William

I have been waiting for what seems like forever. I hate this life, the life that was forced on me. After my brother died, the family business was thrown at me, even though I didn't want it. I'm the sixth generation Hamilton head of the Crown, the British mafia. My job is dangerous, and since I was 22 years old, I had not stopped training in both hand-in-hand combat for defence and offence tactics among other intensive training. I was also told to put up a facade as a University professor. If I were honest to myself, I think the facade was being the head of the Crown. I love teaching at the university; life was simpler - I go in and teach. Having to hide under plain sight is what allows me to escape from drugs, politics, trafficking that I have to deal with. Not a single person was able to trace any of these as we were careful. From all the illegal activities, the Crown, aside from getting involved, has a percentage. A percentage that could feed the entire country for a lifetime.

Terrorism? It happens under my watch.

I can say that the Hamiltons are the *real* Royal Family. My father at the moment, is ill, but when Samuel, my brother, was shot dead by Demyan, the head of the Russian mob, everything's been worse. Demyan is the father of Erika, my late brother's girlfriend, and whom he cheated on. With what happened, my father became gravely ill that requires more medical attention 24/7. It pains me every time I see him like that, but he left me a responsibility, so I have to do this for him and for my family.

My marriage has been arranged the minute Samuel was shot dead. I will be marrying Erika even though it's against my will. I'm not supposed to get married until I turn 35 years old; it's a personal preference that involves Isabel.

I saw her a couple of years ago in a sports event where her husband, Sam Winter, was the highlight of it. She wore something that would make every man's head in the room turn to ogle. She donned on a long, metallic, skin-tight dress, and she was the most beautiful woman I have ever seen. I was told that Sam and Isabel had a daughter, and I must admit, our lives were very different. It wasn't only that occasion that I saw her; I saw her a couple more times. I grew obsessed with her; I would jog around a few yards away from her running trail and have some people keep tabs on her. Her smile was always radiant. She had this innocent look, a naive personality that truly captivated a man like me. I tried to keep my interests within myself, but Demyan started to keep tabs on me as well. To protect her, my interest, I came up with an excuse. I proposed to Sam to throw the game over.

Sam was the easy target. He was vain, selfish, and didn't really value Isabel. The stupid man, in exchange for fame and money, didn't throw the game and decided to prioritise his image than his family. I would give everything just so I can have Isabel and her daughter. Me, her, and her daughter, we would be perfect as family.

Everything went along fine until she stumbled upon Jack Reed. He wasn't part of the plan. I was hurt when she fell in love with Jack, but I didn't falter. I still pursued her despite the odds. To my mafia alliances, I was meeting Isabel to find out if her husband, who now owed us billions on bets, is truly dead. Little did they know that this is one of my plans to date her and see her. But like what I have said, Jack Reed came along, and my plans were ruined. But Isabel will be mine, I will make sure of that.

"Boss. Finley is here to see you," one of my men said.

"Send him in," I said, sitting back on my leather chair.

Finley is a mercenary, the best there is. You can give him a task, and he knows what to do and how to execute it cleanly and silently.

"Hi, boss," Finley said with a wicked smile.

"So, is it done?" I asked.

"Of course. What do you take me for? Are you still doubting my abilities?" he said with an evil smirk.

"No, I don't doubt that for a second. Just want to make sure. Did you run into any trouble?" I asked.

"No. It went as planned," he chuckled. "Mark is no more, and Jack's lads were there as predicted."

"Good," I said feeling satisfied.

"So, what now?" Finley asked.

"Now, we wait."

Finley got up and left. I envisioned Isabel in my head with her beautiful smile, her gaze, the look on her face. . . And then my thoughts were interrupted by a loud ring from my phone. I looked at the caller ID, it was Isabel. I felt happy, butterflies in my stomach like a teenage boy. I answered and made myself sound cool but uninterested with whatever she has to say.

"Isabel, what a wonderful surprise," I said.

"William, I need to speak to you. In person," she said sternly.

I began to become excited but also trying to remember to act nonchalantly.

"Of course, just tell me when and where. Perhaps I can pick you up at home?" I asked.

"No! Just. . . meet me at Natural History Museum tomorrow at 11 am. Don't be late as I don't have much time," she demanded.

"I'll be there, but Isabel, will we have company?" I inquired.

"I might have someone tailing me, but I'll try to lose them," she said.

"They can join us. I have no problem with that," I said, smiling, thinking how uncomfortable she must be feeling.

"Just. . . just don't be late," she said before ending the call.

This is going according to my plan, but I want to prepare as this could be a trap. I called Finley immediately.

"Yes, boss?" he answered.

"Plans have changed. Isabel called me just now. She wants to meet me at the Natural History Museum tomorrow at 11 am. Prepare as she will be with your good friend tailing her. I don't want any interference of prying eyes."

"Leave it to me. You'll know when and where to go when the time comes," he said.

I ended the call feeling anxious and elated to be able to see Isabel finally, and possible be close to her, close enough to maybe kiss her.

I woke up early, feeling excited. I haven't felt like this for a long, long time now. I got myself ready and looked at myself in the wall mirror. I thought I looked sophisticated in my tailored burgundy suit. I have a great physique - I'm tall and bulk from training. My well trimmed bearded gives me an hedge but not too much. This would make a good impression to Isabel, I would say.

I got into my Bugatti and headed off to my destination. When I arrived, the museum was quite busy, full of school groups making some field trips, and tourists tagging along with the long queues. I kept walking around, kept looking for Isabel but to no avail. I received a text message from Finley telling me to take the next right and make my way to a closed-off area. When I approached the exit, a lady opened it for me and gave me a suggestive smile as if she knows me and why I was there. I saw the room, and it was grand and fancy. It was full of gemstones around, and the floor was overlooking the gardens. I approach it to admire and look out and suddenly contemplated how my future would look like with Isabel. I snapped out of it when I heard the voice I've been waiting for.

"You came," Isabel said.

I turned around and she was finally right in front of me.

"Hello, Isabel. Of course, I came," I greeted back while putting my hands inside my trousers' pockets and slowly walking towards her. In all honesty, I was a bit nervous and I could see her getting frightened as I was an inch closer to her.

"Why are you afraid of me, Isabel?" I asked, stopping on my tracks.

She shook her head and stood taller, looking at me with determination before speaking.

"I want to know what do you want for this madness to stop," Isabel asked raising her voice.

"What madness you speak of?" I feigned confusion.

"Well, you know exactly what I mean," she started to cry silently.

My walls came down upon seeing her cry.

"You killed Mark, did you not?" she accused while her eyes were beginning to become angrier and sadder.

Looking at me like that, I hesitated to answer.

"I can't believe you are a monster, William. All the time we were together, you only wanted to know if Sam was alive. How could you? I liked you, William."

I almost choked but answered her immediately, "Sam owes us a lot of money."

"How much? How much money does he owe you? I can pay you, every penny, and more if that is what you want," she said.

She closed her eyes and clenched her tummy as in pain. I came rushing to her side.

"What is it? What's wrong?" I asked worriedly.

She stood up straight and moved out of my reach. "I'm fine," she said.

She wasn't fine. I saw the pain she was feeling moments ago but she didn't really look well, now that I realised.

"You shouldn't have come, Isabel. You are obviously not well," I turned to the window pissed off. I was angry at Jack's mediocre security. This would have never happened if *I* were the one protecting her. I would never leave her side.

"William, just tell me what I have to pay for you to leave my family and me alone," she said.

I was hurt hearing this but resumed to my persona. "What family, Isabel? Sam? Jack?" I chuckled. "They aren't your family. Sam betrayed you in the worst way possible. And Jack. . . Jack is not good enough for you. He left you, too. He can't even keep you protected."

"They were wrong, sure. But they are my family. I beg you. Please, just tell me what you want so you can leave my family alone," she pleaded.

I looked at her sad, desperate eyes, and it almost made me think twice of maybe just give up, but then I was reminded of why I wanted to do this in the first place.

"There's nothing you can do, Isabel. Nothing you are *willing* to do," I said, forming a new maybe even better plan in my head instantly.

"Whatever it is, just tell me. I'll do anything to keep everyone safe again," she said strongly.

I walked around the gemstone exhibition, taking my time. I could feel Isabel's eyes on me. When I came to where she was standing, I looked down at her and brought my hand to her face, she flinched but didn't move away. I was looking into her teary eyes and god I wanted so much to kiss her.

"If you leave them and be mine of your own free will, I will never, ever hurt them," I demanded.

She stepped back shocked at my request.

"What?" she whispered.

"You'll work for me in one of my many companies and will be my mistress. You and your little girl won't ever want for anything. I will provide you a life with everything you desire. Lara's career will be even bigger than what it is now," I said.

"Are you out of your mind?" she said, moving away from me even further.

"Oh no, I'm quite lucid, I can assure you."

"No, William, you are crazy. How can you think I would accept such a demand?" Isabel said.

"That's my proposal to you. I'll forgive and forget Sam's disrespect to us the mafia, and let both Jack and Sam move on with their lives if you choose to accept my proposal. You have my word; no harm will ever come to either of them."

"NO! William, be reasonable. What you are asking me, it's unthinkable. Let me pay you instead to cover Sam's debt and mistake," Isabel proposed.

"I insist on my terms. Pay me by joining me. That's the only payment I accept. If you refuse, I can assure you, you'll lose them both for good," I threatened.

"William, please don't do this," she pleaded, grabbing me by my jacket.

I gently cupped her sweet face with both of my hands.

"You have two weeks to decide what you want to do. You know how to reach me," I said.

"I'm pregnant," she blurted out. "And I'm sick," she looked at me determined.

I saw the truth in her words because of the way she said them. I felt hurt. "No. No," I whispered, unable to accept the truth. "Who's the father?"

"Jack of course," she said, looking away.

I thought to myself, it doesn't matter. I will raise it like my own.

"What's wrong with your health?" I asked.

She looked down at the floor. "Aren't you suppose to all about everything? It's cancer," she said.

I felt overwhelmed by everything she said. I let out a whimper, "No, it can't be."

I paced the huge room now. How could i not know this? Someone would pay for not getting this information.

"So, as you can see, I don't have anything to offer you other than more trouble, which I'm sure isn't exactly how you expected it to be," she said, trying to reason with me.

"How bad is the cancer?" I asked, not stopping at my pacing.

"It's cervical cancer. I'm waiting for the results to come through just to be sure what stage it is. So far, we think it's stage one."

I figured this wouldn't really be a problem. If she chooses to be with me, I can help her. I stopped pacing and came to face her again.

"I can take care of you. I have so many connections, doctors, medical experts, those who can cure you," I said, trying to convince her.

She shook her head. "William, you aren't thinking properly. I have a child from Sam, and I have another one on the way from Jack. I also have cervical cancer. How can you still want me?"

"Because. . . Isabel. . ." I was about to tell her that I was in love with her, but I thought it wasn't the right time. If I tell her now, she might use it against me, and I can't do that.

". . . That is the payment. Take it or leave it. See the people you love live longer, and you get cured of your situation now, or you lose them and die, too," I said, trying to sound cold.

"But William, all that I wish for are not possessions. It's to have the people I love around me."

"And you will have. Your children," I said, as a matter of fact.

"William, please don't do this," she still continued to plead.

"As I have said, you don't have to give me the answer right now. You have two weeks from today," I kissed her cheek before leaving the room.

My thoughts were racing as fast as my heart. She'll be mine after all and on her own free will. I was so happy I could burst. I was smiling ear to ear as I got inside my car. It won't be long now, it won't be too long at all. All I have to do now is arrange what she'll need. The doctors, the house, work. . . everything. She will grow to love me, and she will fall for me as I have fallen for her. I should tread carefully about Demyan, though. I'll have to be discreet it has to appear as I keep Isabel against her will. I'll have to be, at least, careful until Erika and I get married so I can gain Demyan's trust.

CHAPTER 14

Isabel

I was ultimately shocked after meeting William. After everything he has put us through, he still wants us to endure even more. How could I ever accept his proposal? It wasn't also a proposal but more like an ultimatum? How can I bring my children into such a wicked relationship? Yes, it will become a relationship, or slavery - whatever you prefer to call it. It's degrading and won't bring happiness to me. I don't understand why he would want this. . . this kind of arrangement. He seemed worried about me for a minute but then maltreats me as if I was his property and inhumanely. This man is disgusting, a chauvinist, and a cold mafia goon.

I broke my thoughts and started walking towards the exit of the building when strong hands grabbed me to the side.

"Where the fuck were you?" Jack's eyes were wild, he was visibly shaking. He was freakishly pale.

"I. . . I got lost," I whispered.

He didn't buy it. The look on his face, he was clearly not convinced with my excuse.

"Let's go home. We'll talk in the car," he said, looking around.

I noticed that while we were walking, there were many security guards that surrounded us. Alex had a heated exchange with someone I didn't recognise.

There was no trace of William in the building. I was still thinking about him and what he said. He has this intimidating figure with a cold voice and stares. I shook myself before getting inside the car.

"Where were you, Isabel? What happened to you? Why did you give the slip to Alex?" Jack furiously asked.

I didn't look at him. I was still drowned in my thoughts that I didn't notice I wasn't able to answer him in time.

"Isabel!" he shouted.

"Just leave me alone, Jack. I don't want to talk about it," I said without looking at him.

"Oh no, you don't. You are going to tell me. This is not a joke, Isabel. I'm serious. You were in danger. You put yourself in danger. Why?" Jack insisted on asking me.

A tear suddenly fell down my cheek, but I wiped it as soon as my hand met it. "You don't own me, Jack. I can do whatever I want," I said.

Jack was quiet for a while, and then he blurted, "I thought I lost you back there. I actually thought I wouldn't be able to find you or worst find you lying dead on the cold floor. Do you realise that you had me worried sick?" he said, trying to hold back his frustration and anger.

I looked at him and found his cheeks were wet with his own tears. He brought his head to his hands, trying to get a hold of himself but failing. I grabbed his head and brought it to my chest and felt his quiet sobs.

"I'm sorry, Jack. I'm so sorry," I said sobbing.

I thought that it would be impossible to leave him. It will kill him., but I have to protect him and Sam, too. And the only way to do that is to accept what William proposed. He controls everything, and there is no other way out of this. How will I tell him that I will have to leave him for good? He'll lose his mind knowing that he'll no longer be taking care of our baby and me.

When we arrived home, we were still crying. Jack opened the car, and we went inside straight to our bedroom. He crashed his lips onto mine, kissing me ever so passionately. He didn't even hold back. He grabbed my hair and pulled back to allow him better access to my neck.

"You said I didn't own you," he said while kissing me. He took off my jacket and ripped my button-down shirt. I whimpered a little, not sure if I was afraid, or it was because of the desire I felt. My emotions were all over the place right now. When he pulled down my skinny jeans, he kneeled in front of me and grabbed my leg, bringing it over his shoulder. He pulled my lacy panty to one side and started to spontaneously licked my clit with his tongue. He then moved up and down, leaving me panting. My nipples were so hard they were actually hurting wanting to have a little attention with his fondle. I was really close to climaxing when he got up and turned my back to him, kissing along my neck, then my shoulder. He spun me around again, and I only realised that I didn't have my bra on when he captured my nipple with his hot, wet lips, licking with his warm tongue. I moaned so loud.

"I own you," he said.

"You are mine. Never forget that," he said before capturing my mouth again.

How I wanted this to be true. I felt I was his, but I was afraid that this was an illusion or a dream that wouldn't last.

Jack grabbed his tie and tied my left wrist to the bed's frame.

"If you ever decide to give Alex or any other security detail for that matter, the slip this is what I will do. I will tie you to the bed," he said.

I didn't mind being in this position. He can tie me for as long as he wanted. If this were the way he treats me, I would be happy and welcome it.

Jack stripped down his clothes and grabbed my waist, turning me around, making me kneel. He opened my legs wider and stood back, looking at me. I looked over my shoulder to see what he was doing, and I saw his penis erected. He saw me looking, and he started to stroke it, closing his eyes briefly. That made me so wet, my knees shook with desire. My breathing became erratic, and so is my heart. He brought his penis, his entire manhood, to my now-wet clit, rubbing against it with its head. The friction and speed made me reach closer to the climax. He continued this until I felt that I was about to come. When I climaxed, he was inside me, pumping every last bit out of me. He laid me down on my back and brought my legs over his shoulders and entered me again, grinding my clit with his pelvis. We groaned and moaned, and it became louder. The smell of sex was all over; it was increasingly aphrodisiac as the moments go by. We finally came together, but I felt a slight pain. I wasn't sure if it was because of his huge dick, or maybe it was because I was sick from cancer, but everything felt good even the pain. Suddenly, William's words echoed in my mind.

"That's the payment. Take it or leave it. See the people you love live their lives as they are supposed to, and you get cured of cancer or lose them, and you might die, too."

I thought of everyone I love - my mum, Lizzy, Lara, Jack. Lizzy needs me now more than ever, so how can I leave?

I looked at Jack as he placed gentle kisses on my shoulder and drew little circles on my tummy.

How can I leave Jack? How can I live my life without him? This will ruin his life. Him losing me, Lara, and his own unborn child. There must be another way. Think Isabel. Think. I need to speak to Alex.

"What are you thinking about, Isabel?" Jack asked.

I shook my head slightly and gave him a small smile.

"Nothing important," I said, convincing him to believe me.

"Please don't lie to me. I know something happened back at the museum. Something you didn't like. If you don't tell me, I won't be able to protect you, baby," he said.

I closed my eyes as I felt Jack closer to my face. I felt useless because I can't tell him about William. I can't tell him that I met him at the museum. He wouldn't understand.

"Jack. . ." I said, thinking about what to tell him.

"I really don't want to talk about it. Can you trust me and just leave it be, please," I pleaded.

He looked into my eyes, trying to decide whether he would drop it or insist. He must have seen the desperation because he closed his eyes, nodded to the agreement, and kissed me on the forehead gently. I knew he held it in as he wanted to respect my decision. This will give me enough time to speak to Alex and find another way to figure this out.

Later that night, I woke up finding Jack holding me tight. I slowly took his arm away; he budged but didn't wake up. Ever so quietly, I left the bedroom and went to check on Lara. She was sound asleep, so I went downstairs and to the kitchen. To my surprise, Lizzy was in the kitchen and in the dark with a cup of coffee in front of her.

"Lizzy, are you okay?" I asked, concerned for her.

"Yeah. I just couldn't sleep," she said quietly.

I hugged her tight, trying to comfort her, and kissed her head before I headed to the coffee maker to get coffee for myself.

"Jack's making all the funeral arrangements. I hope that is okay with you," I said.

"Of course, it is. I can't thank you both enough for what you are doing for me," Lizzy said.

"Lizzy, this is nothing. To be honest, I feel partly responsible for Mark's death," I said sadly.

"What? Stop. Don't even start, Isabel. Mark made his decisions. It wasn't anyone's fault but those mafia bastards," she replied.

"Lizzy, you know I love you, right?" I said, holding her hand.

"Of course, I do Isabel. I love you, too. What's wrong?" she asked.

I shook my head. "Nothing. I just need you to know that. No matter what happens, I want you to know I will always think of you as my sister and my best friend. I would do anything for you, no matter where I am, okay?"

Lizzy looked into my eyes and became worried.

"Isabel, what's going on? I know you, and I can feel that something's not right."

"No, no. I just need you to know how much you mean to me, that's all."

I could see she wasn't convinced, but she didn't insist.

"Okay," she said, holding my other hand while squeezing it firmly.

"I think I will go to bed now," she said, dropping a kiss on my cheek before leaving.

Yet again, I felt lost. Alex wasn't around, so I can't really do anything. It was a dreadful night, but I decided to sleep it off.

In the morning, Jack kissed me on the cheek, waking me up.

"Good morning, Mr. Reed," I whispered.

"Say that again," he whispered back happily.

I giggled, "Are you going to the office today?"

"No. We are going to get the biopsy results today," he said as if reminding me.

God, I totally forgot about that, so I let out a sigh.

"I need to get breakfast ready," I said.

"No you don't," he said, moving over me.

"Yes, I do," I insisted.

"Yesterday, while you were *disobedient,* I was interviewing a housekeeper who will work full time with us. I think you will like her," he said, excited to break the news to me.

"What? No," I said, disappointed with his decision. "Jack, I told you about this before. I don't need a housekeeper. I can do everything, and I don't need help."

"Isabel, now with your illness and Lara's schedule, Lizzy's situation, and this whole thing with Sam, we both know you need help around here. Dr. Shelly said you need a lot of rest and less stress as these would make you and the baby healthy. That's what we are going to do."

I didn't know what to say because he was right. There was so much going on that I don't know how I will cope with it. I finally agreed and supported his decision.

"Fine. But if I want to cook, I will," I said, pointing my finger at him.

He captured my finger between his teeth playfully as if he was biting it before answering

"Of course. You are the boss."

"I would love to think so," I said, pushing him away from atop of me.

"Noooo. Don't go," he pleaded.

"I need to wake Lara up because she needs to do some school work," I said.

"Fine. I'll have to go and meet the funeral home manager to go over the plan. Do you want to tag along?" he asked.

"No, I need to help Lara with her school work," I said, smacking his lips with mine.

He put on a suit and left. This is the perfect opportunity for me to speak to Alex in private. When I got to the kitchen, Sofia, who was our part-time housekeeper, was there putting breakfast on the table.

"Sofia?" I called.

"Ola, Isabel," she greeted me.

I went to hug her. "Jack got you working full time?"

"Yes, he was very persuasive. Besides, I think this would the best place for me to work. In this way, I don't have to drive around from one house to the next," she said happily.

I figured Jack must have offered her a great pay but knowing him, he must have convinced Sofia to get her working full time.

"I'm so glad it was you," I said.

"Oh, that's great! I was hoping you would like the idea," Jack said from behind me.

I thought he already left, so I turned and hugged him and kissed his lips.

"I couldn't ask for better help," I said, looking to Sofia.

"Now if you will excuse me, I need to wake Lara up and get her ready."

"She's already awake, and she is almost ready," Sofia said immediately.

"What? Did you do that?" I asked her.

"Of course. I have been up since 6 am. There wasn't much to do, so I assumed Lara needed to go to school. I hope it's okay," she said, a bit worried about doing things ahead.

"Of course, it's okay, Sofia. She's not going to school this week but needs to do some school work. That's great that you woke her up before I did," I replied.

"I'm happy to help, Isabel. Just tell me if there is anything you need," she said with a kind smile.

"I told Sofia about your condition. She needed to know in case you get ill, and she's there to help when I'm not around," Jack said after taking a sip of his coffee.

"I understand," I said, not looking at Sofia as I didn't want to see her face pitying me.

"Good morning, everyone," Lara greeted, kissing me first.

"Good morning, darling. How was your sleep?" I asked.

"Good. How are you feeling, mummy?"

"Better," I said, smiling at her to reassure her.

"Cool. Mummy, today, I need to go to the studio. Can I take Hayley with me? She's dying to see me recording my songs, and today, we are going to record a new song with a new artist Jack signed into his label."

I looked at Jack, and he answered her back. "Of course, darling. We'll pick her up from school and take you to eat something first. We'll then head off to the studio."

This is perfect. Jack will be out most of the day, which will give me enough time to speak with Alex and device a plan with him.

Around 11 am, I got a call from Dr. Shelly, and as expected, the biopsy results were positive for stage 1 cancer. This didn't really affect me or anything. I was prepared and expected it. Dr. Shelly advised that I will be making monthly appointments to do blood works, scans, and urine samples to keep an eye on the growth and development of my illness. Jack wasn't really happy about my decision, but it was my body, after all. I knew I wouldn't forgive myself if I go through an abortion. I know how precious a gift the baby was, and I wasn't about to lose this opportunity to hold my baby in my arms.

"Lara, come down. It's time to go pumpkin," Jack called from the bottom of the staircase. He then came into the living room where I was sitting with Lizzy going over the arrangements Jack has done for Mark's funeral.

"We'll be back around 7 pm tonight, baby," Jack said before dropping a kiss on my cheek.

"Okay. Can you grab a fresh French baguette on the way, please?" I asked before he left.

He nodded. Lara came in and kissed me goodbye and hugged Lizzy tight. "Will you be all right, Aunt Lizzy?" she asked.

"Of course, honey. Go on and make us proud, okay? Bring me a copy of your recording, will you?" Lizzy requested. She sounded better, but not totally.

"She resembles you," Lizzy told me.

"Yeah? How so?" I asked, not sure in what way.

"She worries a lot for the people she loves," she said, giving me a small smile.

"I wish I could be as calm as she is, though. She seems to have dealt a lot of stress lately, but she is managing it well. I can't believe she's only nine," I said.

"We all have a way of dealing with things. I would normally freak out in situations like this," Lizzy said, laughing a bit.

"Yeah, and I would normally cry, bawling my eyes out," I added.

We both laughed at what we said. Lizzy looked at me, and I saw the sadness in her eyes. It brought me tears, too.

"Lizzy, you are the strongest person I know. If I was able to move on with my life after I learned of Sam's. . ." I closed my eyes, recalling the worst days I had when they broke the news to me that Sam died.

"I don't know if I will be able to move on, Isabel. Mark was my life. Even after I found out he had given information to the Crown about you, I still couldn't let him go. Should I be able to let him go now?" she said, trying not to cry by getting up and pacing the room.

"You will. You have so many people around you who love you, Lizzy. You have us," I said, but feeling guilty instantly because I didn't know if I would be really there for her.

"I know, I know. It's just. . . I feel like I'm not complete anymore. Something is missing right here," she said, putting her hand on her chest.

I got up and hugged her close to me and whispered into her ear, "I know the feeling. I can't promise it will ever go away, but what I can promise is that it will get better." I really tried comforting her by hugging her tightly.

"Thank you for everything, Isabel. The funeral will be a beautiful goodbye, thanks to Jacks' and your hard work."

"It's the least we could do. Now, please stay with us for as long as you want. This is your home, too," I said.

Lizzy shook her head before answering, "Thank you, but after the funeral, I want to move back home. I need to be close to Mark somehow, and our home is where I think I would feel connected to him."

"As you wish, Lizzy," I said.

After all the details of the funeral were ironed out, Lizzy went to lie down, and I went to look for Alex. He was in Jack's office, having a meeting with someone virtually. I came to open the door, and he bid goodbye to the person he was talking to on the computer, "Yes, we'll be in touch when he calls us."

The person he talked to responded, "Great, but Alex, this has to be kept between us until everything has been settled. I don't want anything to jeopardise the mission."

"Of course, I have to go now. But we'll keep in touch," Alex ending the call and closed his laptop.

"Any update I need to know about?" I asked him.

"No, nothing you need to worry about," he said, scrambling through the desk.

"Alex, I need your help. What I'm about to tell you shouldn't reach Jack no matter what," I told him and waited for his confirmation.

He suddenly frowned.

"Alex, promise me you won't tell Jack about this," I said, leaning closer to the desk while I was on my chair.

"Isabel, if this has something to do with Sam's case, you know he has to know, and I have to tell him about it. We have a huge plan, and anything that involves Sam's issue, it could jeopardise the entire thing. That is why he needs to know," he said.

"You mustn't tell him. I'm begging you. This can change everything. But I can't do this alone. That's why I came to you to ask for your help. Jack's life doesn't need to be in danger. . . I think," I said, feeling less sure now that I saw how serious everything was.

"Okay, just tell me what is going on, and then I tell you if this is something Jack should know about."

"Fine," I said, a bit frustrated and scared at the same time.

"Yesterday, I went to meet with William," I started.

Alex gasped and was shocked. He leaned back into his chair and looked at me with confusion and surprise.

"I know what you are thinking. It was dangerous. But I had to try something, at least. Nobody knows what he really wants, right?"

"You're right. We all needed to know what he wants, and we have a plan for how we could find that out," he continued.

"Jack was supposed to arrange a meeting to discuss it." Alex blurted, "What on earth made you do that call, Isabel? Not only was it dangerous, but it was also stupid! If Jack knows about this, he'll go ballistic."

I closed my eyes briefly, thinking about how Jack could lose his shit if he finds out about this.

"That's why you won't tell him about it," I said, looking serious.

"You better tell me everything you are planning about, Isabel, because this is bad," Alex said worriedly.

I took a deep breath and told him everything. By the time I was finished, Alex was speechless. He got up from his chair and walked back and forth at a fast pace. He turned his back at me, placing one hand on the window frame clearly lost in his deep thoughts.

"Alex, say something," I said.

He shook his head. "So his price is you. . ." he said quietly.

"No, not just me but my children, too. I don't see any way out of this, Alex. If I want both Jack and Sam safe, I need to accept his proposal," I said sadly.

"No, of course, you won't. Jack will never allow this," he said, looking back at me.

"I don't really have any other choice. I have less than two weeks to give him an answer," I said, desperate for Alex to find another way.

"Okay, okay. . . that will give us enough time to come up with a plan. . . or follow through the existing plan, so nothing changes."

"What do you mean nothing changes? We know what he wants. He won't meet with Jack now, and even if he does, he will tell Jack about his proposal, and Jack will refuse it and in the process he gets killed," I said, feeling more and more scared.

"No, Isabel. What you don't know is that we are working with an MI5 team. They are a special team we tapped into who will be present at Jack's meeting with William. We'll take him down then," Alex said, explaining.

"Alex. . . are you crazy? Do you really think this will work? If they had anything on William, they would have got him already."

"That's why we need him to meet Jack, and he will get William to admit that he's the head of the Crown. They have all the evidence they need — the last piece of the puzzle is knowing who is behind the Crown."

I was starting to see where the plan was going. I found a bit of hope with the plan they have in place.

"Do you think this will work?" I asked quietly.

"I think our chances are good. But we can't leave anything to chance. Two weeks will help us devise a new plan to get William. Isabel, I think Jack should know about your meeting with William," Alex insisted.

"No. If this plan works, then there's no need for him to get upset over nothing, right?"

"I guess. Just promise me you won't do such a thing again, okay?" he asked seriously.

"I won't, I promise. Alex, please. Please try to get William because I don't know what I would do if I had to accept his proposal. If this plan of yours doesn't work, I will have no choice but to accept his demands just to get Jack and Sam safe from him."

"We won't let that happen," Alex said with determination.

I nodded and left the study feeling a bit more confident that everything would work out.

CHAPTER 15

Jack

Isabel has been very strange since she came from the museum. I can't seem to put my finger on it, but she has been quiet as if she is contemplating. It could be all the things that are happening at the moment, but I have a feeling it's something else. She's hiding something from me, and I can't figure out what it is.

"Jack, the cars are outside waiting," Alex said from the study doorway.

Today is Mark's funeral. The mood in the house has been miserable. Even Lara's wonderful, cheerful personality can't cover the atmosphere we had.

As I went to get Isabel from the master bedroom, I heard a bit of a conversation she was having with Lizzy.

"Remember when we went to the Maldives when Sam had his first big win?" Isabel said.

"Yes," Lizzy chuckled a little and remembered, "Mark and I had been engaged for a few months, and he thought he would arrange that "Supposed Romantic" hike to the highest point on Mount Villingili."

"Yes, Sam and I had to send a search party to find you because you got lost for 36 hours," Lizzy and Isabel laughed.

We needed to leave, but since they have seemed to enjoy the conversation, I opted to wait for just a little longer.

"We have had amazing times together, haven't we?" Isabel said.

"Yes," Lizzy sniffled a little.

"We'll get through this. Let us say goodbye to Mark, remembering the good times we have had, okay?" Isabel said, trying to comfort Lizzy.

I thought this was my cue, so I entered the room, and they both looked my way. Isabel looked pale.

"The car is ready, we must go," I told them.

As Lizzy went past me, I kissed her cheek to comfort her. Isabel took a deep breath and gave me a small smile when I held out my hand to her.

"Are you okay? You're looking pale. Do you feel pain?"

"I feel a bit nauseated, but it'll pass," she said.

Every time I see her struggle either because of pregnancy or the illness, my heart tightens up as I feel sorry for her.

The funeral went well, I have written a small speech for Mark, and so did Isabel who broke down into tears half-way through her speech. She was able to finish reading it; she's a strong woman. The shock we got was from the unexpected guest. Alex rushed to me and whispered into my ear, "William is here with a group of his men."

I turned my head so fast. "What?"

Alex pressed his hand to his earpiece and looked at me again before saying, "He's coming this way, probably to speak to Lizzy."

"How dare he," I whispered, getting pissed.

"That bastard killed Mark. How can he have the audacity to show up?" I asked Alex.

"Listen, tell Isabel now. I'll take care of Lizzy," Alex directed.

I nodded and I grabbed Isabel's arm, taking her away slightly from Lizzy while Alex spoke to her.

"Isabel, William's here, and he's coming this way," I whispered to Isabel.

"No. . ." she said visibly scared. I saw panic in her eyes. She quickly turned to Lizzy, who was now crying but was also trying to hold her tears. Alex had her against his chest, whispering in her ear. Isabel rushed to Lizzy.

"I'm here. I'm here, Lizzy," she said, rubbing Lizzy's arms.

"Remember, don't react. That's what William wants you to do," Alex reminded her.

"How can she not react, Alex? This is fucked up," I whispered louder and angrily.

"Remember about the plan. Just stick to it," he reminds me again. I swallowed a hard lump in my throat, trying to hold back my frustration.

William was dressed in a very, very dark burgundy suit, it was almost black. He had a black rose in the pocket of his suit. He gave me a little nod with a smile on his lips before turning to Lizzy.

"My deepest condolences, Mrs. McNeal. Mark and I were very close colleagues. He has helped me a lot over the years.

That was big enough to get a reaction from us, but I held back and bit my tongue. Isabel was holding, gripped my hand, but she was shaking from anger. She was dodging to look at William, poor thing, scared out of her mind.

"Thank you, William," Lizzy said with a shaken voice but was also holding herself in check.

William kissed Lizzy's cheeks, and I noticed Alex flexed his fists, and his jaw was locked. He was ready to spring on William when necessary. What took me back was when William turned to Isabel and addressed her the way he did.

"Hello again, sweet Isabel. How are you feeling?" William asked.

Isabel looked up to William, and her pale face got even paler if that was even possible. He then bent and whispered something in her ear, just before I stepped closer to her.

"I think it's time for you to leave," I said, anger starting to take over me, and I pushed him back slightly away from Isabel, who was now looking at William with wild eyes from whatever he had said to her.

I reminded William again to leave.

"You know how to find me," he said to Isabel, giving me one last smug look that I wanted immediately to punch out of him.

As I gave one step forward, Alex stopped me. This was so fucking hard, knowing who this bastard is, what he did, and what he was capable of, yet I was unable to do anything about it.

On our way back to the house, Isabel was avoiding me, keeping herself busy with Lizzy and Lara talking about small things such as how lovely the flowers looked and how beautiful the whole ceremony was. Every time I would catch her eye, she would avert her look immediately, which was a tell-tale that she was, in fact, hiding something from me.

My insides wore twisting, remembering William's words to her. They have been in contact, and I was afraid it was because of what happened in the museum. This was all my fault, how could I not see this coming? Isabel is very protective of her loved ones, of course, she would try and resolve this on her own, but she does't how dangerous this can get.

Even at home, she was avoiding me. But I wouldn't let this go. She will have to explain everything to me, so I waited for her sitting in the bedroom armchair while I sipped on my whiskey. It was probably a bad idea to drink one that night because I was getting furious with Isabel for putting herself in danger. When she entered the bedroom, she didn't bother saying a word and went to bed. I didn't move from where I was either as I was waiting for her to take notice of me. When she laid down on the bed and turned her bedside lamp off, I snapped.

"Really?" I said, looking her way, but she didn't say or do anything.

"You really think I would just leave you be after William's little scene?" I asked, getting up and sitting next to her on the bed.

Isabel slowly moved up the bed and sat against the bed headboard.

"No, but I was hoping you would," she said.

"Hoping is not enough, Isabel," I said.

She nodded a little, she looked at me, and I saw the sadness in her eyes. Such sadness that with that look, I wanted to let it go and give in to her. But I closed my eyes briefly to gather myself up. I got up and took the last gulp of my drink, letting the liquid burn all the way down before speaking.

"Don't you trust me, Isabel?" I asked.

"Of course, I do, Jack," she replied.

"So why won't you tell me what's going on?"

"Because. . . because this is my problem, not yours," she said.

It pissed me off; how could she say such a thing? Everything that has to do with her and Lara *was* my problem. I shook my head and turned away from her

"Is that really how you see it?" i said. She didn't answer.

"Isabel, look at me!" I shouted.

She looked at me, surprised that I shouted at her.

"You have a plan, so follow it. Nothing has changed." She ventures.

"Nothing has changed? You're wrong. Everything has changed, including you," I pointed at her.

My temper was growing even more out of control. There were a lot of things I wanted to say, but the words wouldn't come out properly.

"You keep on making decisions that affects me without talking to me. You used to talk to me about everything. We would never hide anything from each other. You've changed, Isabel."

"Well, people change. Maybe all this time I had to endure all of this things, made me change. Or maybe this is who I am, after all. I don't need anyone to solve my problems. I can deal with them myself," she said, looking straight at me.

It hurts hearing this more than I could ever imagine.

"You don't mean that, Isabel."

"Of course, I do," she said, without regretting it.

We stood there looking at each other. Neither one of us wavering in our resolve.

"What did he tell you in the museum?" I asked, referring to William.

"I have already told you that this is my problem. I'm sick and tired of people trying to sort my problems out. Maybe this plan of yours will never work. Maybe I need to deal with it myself."

"Don't you dare do anything stupid. Are you listening? I won't allow you to mess this up. I'll make sure we are all out of danger, and William ends up behind bars," I said, furious and frustrated at her for even thinking of doing something about this.

Isabel laughed sarcastically. "You don't even know what he wants."

"I don't need to know what he wants. I just need to arrange a meeting, and when he admits that he wants Sam dead, he's going down."

"You are delusional, Jack, if you think you can get William to talk. What about his connections? The Russian mafia? Do you really think that they will just let it go if you get William arrested? What did they do with that mercenary that works for them? He was supposed to be in jail, but he's a free man committing horrible crimes. Do you think William will remain in jail for long?" she presented to me all the facts that I already know.

In the back of my mind, these were concerns I had but have never spoken about. Maybe because I hoped and believed that the plan would work, she must have seen my face because she looked away with a sad smile.

"It has been a long day. I need to rest," she said finally.

I stood there without moving for a while but feeling so mad that I changed into my workout clothes and went for a run. Alex was beside me quicker than I thought.

"You make me look so out of shape, you know," I complimented him without looking his way.

"To be fair, you actually look quite good. I have many years of extreme training," he said, trying to keep our conversation light.

We ran for about six miles, lost in my thoughts. I spoke to Alex, "Alex, she's hiding something from me. Find out what it is."

"Jack, I think when she's ready, she'll tell you. Trust me," he said, making me a bit more suspicious.

"You know what it is, don't you? You know what William wants," I said, stopping to look at him.

He nodded, confirming my suspicion.

"Jack, nothing has changed. If I believed it would affect the plan, I would tell you right away."

"Alex, her safety is my priority. I need to know everything so I can protect her," I said firmly.

"I'm sorry, Jack. Isabel made me promise not to tell you anything. This is something very personal for her."

"Not even if I dismiss you?" I said, angry for not being able to know what is going on.

"My word is very important. She doesn't think I should tell you. Again, I made a promise. I'm sorry, Jack," he said.

I shook my head and screamed at the Thames River in front of me.

"I FEEL SO FUCKING USELESS!" I shouted.

"Don't be. The plan will work," Alex comforted me by patting me on the back.

"No, it won't, Alex. Who are we kidding? You know the chances of it," I said.

Alex didn't show any worry, but I was sure he felt it.

"There are lots of other things we'll be doing to get everyone safe once William has been put away," he said.

"No, we can't run from the reality. I need to know what William wants and try to figure out how we can give it to him."

Alex closed his eyes and pressed his thumb into his nose bridge.

"It's impossible to give him what he wants," Alex said hopelessly.

"Alex, you can't keep his demands from me. How can I protect my family if I don't know what his demands are?"

"Jack, just trust me that we can keep everyone protected one way or another," Alex said, who has already made up his mind.

I looked away from him because I knew he wouldn't tell me anyway. I thought to myself of finding another way for Isabel to open up to me or someone she trusts that I can talk about this.

"Let us go back before Isabel starts to worry," Alex said.

I nodded, and on my way back, the image of William's smug smile flashed before me. I couldn't live like this, always afraid for the people I love. Isabel will have to tell me, no matter what. No matter what.

CHAPTER 16

Sam

My mistakes haunted me like the dark of the night. Everywhere I looked, I see what I lost, what I had, what I could have had if I would just think of the people I love more than myself. Yes, I see it now. I know that I wasn't thinking of Isabel or Lara as I thought. I was thinking of how I would be seen as a loser and a failure to them — what a fucking mess I made. I'm still lying to the woman I said to love for as long as I remember. I left my family not just once but twice.

I looked at a picture I carry with me on my wallet of a petit, long, dark-haired woman with a slightly swollen belly. She looks so happy, so unworried, so different from the last time I saw her. I can't get rid of that image from my head, her tear-stained cheeks, her swearing and shouts of disbelief at me, telling her I had to leave. God, what am I doing? Why do I keep hurting the people I love the most? There's something very wrong with me, which is not normal. I put the picture away and go for a swim in the crystal clear water in the sea and try not to think about the mess I caused. As I was coming out of the sea, my security detail Paul came to me.

"Sam, we need to talk," I nodded and followed him into the beach hut where we were staying at. I sat in the corner sofa in the small open plan living room.

"What is up?" I said, feeling fed up for being cooped up on this island for almost two months.

"I just had a call from Alex, and what he told me has come as a shock. Alex thinks you need to be filled in, but. . ." Paul

165

stopped himself before carrying on. "What I'm about to tell you has to be kept between you and me, Jack can't find out. At least for now."

"Okay, carry on then," I urged him, curious to find out what is so important that the very people who Jack contracted to protect us don't want him to find out.

"Isabel had a meeting last week with William without anyone knowing, and she found out what he wants."

"He wants my head, that's quite clear, isn't it?" I asked, chuckling a little.

"That's what we all thought."

"Are you going to tell me what he wants, or do you want me to guess?" I said, frustrated at his hesitation.

"He wants Isabel. He wants her as his mistress," I was prepared to hear anything at this point, but what he said. . . This was definitely not it.

"What are you talking about? What *the fuck* are you saying?" I was trying to process the information. It didn't make any sense, this couldn't be true.

"He demanded Isabel be his mistress, and everyone else who she cares about will be safe to live their lives as they please."

"She didn't agree to this, did she? Please tell me she didn't," he shook his head before saying. "She asked Alex for advice, and he convinced her not to except. We are going through with the plan we have together with MI5, so she won't need to."

"She won't need to. I would never allow that. I will give myself up before she would even think of such a thing."

I thought to myself this mess is worse than before.

"Look, Sam. Alex just thought you should know because, in a rare case, the plan doesn't go smoothly; you are aware of what he wants. I'm sure everything will work out, but at least you know what is going on."

"Thanks. Why doesn't Alex want to tell Jack, though?" I asked, not understanding why Alex would keep this from Jack.

"Because Isabel made him promise not to tell Jack. Jack can be a hot-headed guy when it comes to his family. . ." he stopped himself realising he was treating *my family* as Jack's. It hurts to hear people referring to the girls as someone else's. But they are right, too. I lost the right to call them mine a long time ago. I pretend that his statement didn't affect me.

"So why tell *me* this?"

"She never said anything about keeping it from you so, Alex just thought best to let you know."

This brought me down even further. She probably didn't even think of me in an equation here.

How could I blame her? She has moved on. She moved on to a better man than I ever was or will be. I need to tell her. I need her to know everything. I got up and walked to my bedroom to make the most difficult call I have ever made. The phone rang and rang, and I was losing hope of Isabel answering when she finally did.

"Hello?" her voice was small and unsure. Then I understood why. I was calling from a private number.

"Oh, hi, Isabel. It's Sam," I said. I hear a long sigh on the other side of Isabel.

"You, okay?" she asked a little more relax.

"Yes, and no," I was starting to lose my nerve, but I needed her to know because it's important for our relationship whatever that is.

"Which is it, Sam?"

"No, I'm not fine. Not until you know the truth," I said.

"The truth? About what Sam?"

"I have been keeping something from you, but you deserve to know," I took a deep breath and carry on.

"While I was in Venezuela, I met someone. Her name was Mariana, and she was a village girl. We got involved, and things got pretty serious really quick. Next thing I knew, she was pregnant. At first, it was like a dream. I was beginning to be happy again, but every time I looked at her, I saw your face and Lara's little dimpled cheeks. All the moments we had together were the only thing I can remember. I cheated on you, and the realisation of my actions started to haunt me, so I told her about you and Lara and told her I had to leave."

Up to this point, Isabel hasn't said a word, so I carried on.

"When I left, she was six months pregnant, and I haven't gotten in touch with her ever since," I finished.

I was beginning to think the phone line was dead as for the long silence when Isabel spoke.

"I really don't know you, do I?" she asked with a sad trembling voice. It hurts so bad to know I betrayed her this way after everything else I put her through.

"I'm so sorry, sorry, Isabel. I didn't want to hurt you, I swear. I fucked up," I said, feeling a lump in my throat, and my eyes stung with tears.

"I have done everything for you, Sam. I have loved you more than myself. How could you have done this to me? To Lara? To that poor woman and her baby?" she said, raising her voice now with anger.

"You don't deserve my forgiveness, my sacrifice. You are even worst than William, who asked me to be his mistress. Yes, you are far worst than him because you destroyed my life, our daughter's life, the people you said you loved. At least William is destroying people's lives that he doesn't feel anything for, but you. . . you say you love us and destroy us over and over again," she said, shouting.

"You're right. I'm a fucking bastard. I don't deserve you or Lara, but I never stopped loving you. Mariana filled a void in my heart. I know I have done a lot of wrong things, but I know it's not yet late. I can make sure they are well-cared for. I will make it right, I promise," I said, desperate to fix all the mess I have done.

"No, Sam. You can never fix this. You broke that woman's heart as you broke mine - that you can never fix. You abandoned her with an unborn child, you abandoned us, how stupid can you be?"

She was right. I was an animal. How could I ever fix this?

"I'm sorry," the hot tears came down my face fast and furious. I grabbed my hair while sitting at the bottom of my bed.

"I did make the right decision. You can never be the man Lara and I deserve. You aren't even fit to be a father."

"Please, Isabel. Don't say that. I love Lara more than anything, please don't take her away from me," I said, desperate now.

"I didn't make that decision, Sam. *You did*. You decided you were no longer her father when you faked your death and stayed away for five years," she said, and ended the call.

I roared and threw the mobile against the wall.

"Fuck!!!" How could a person that has everything in life lose it all? I thought I had nothing before but now. . . now I lost every single thing in my life. Having Isabel as a friend and mother of my daughter would be enough for me, but I lost that right, too.

Everything was going through my head. Why did Isabel, Lara, Jack be responsible for our safety that I messed up? I need to hand myself to William. I had nothing to lose anyway. I just needed to arrange an income stream for Mariana and the baby, and I'll hand myself in.

I called Alex, and he answered almost instantly.

"Sam?" Alex said.

"Hi Alex, can you talk?"

"Just a second," he said, putting me on hold for a second.

"Go ahead," he said.

"Alex, I made a decision, and I need you to help me with this," I said taking a deep breath before continuing.

"I need to get back to England and hand myself to William. This will be better for everyone, and Jack won't have to put himself in danger."

"Why can't anyone stick to the bloody plan. Sam, we already went over this a million times before. Don't make me repeat myself over and over."

"Alex, Paul told me about William's demands and knowing Isabel, believe me when I say she's considering it. No matter what she told you, she'll put the people she loves before her respect and happiness, even her own life, so before she gets the chance, I need to end this, no matter the cost. They deserve this Alex, after everything I put them through after I have betrayed them, this is the least I can do," I said.

I heard Alex exhaled loudly.

"Look, you are right. They do deserve this, but we believe this plan will work. So let us just give it a shot first, and if it doesn't work, then we look for alternatives, alright?" he said.

"Alex, why lose time, resources, and bring unnecessary danger to Jack? I just hand myself in, and it all ends."

"No, it won't. William was very clear, he doesn't want you. He wants Isabel. Just let us do our job and try this first," Alex said firmly.

"Fine," I groaned. "This better work, because if it doesn't, you will bring me back to England," I said before ending the call.

CHAPTER 17

Isabel

I was locked in the bathroom, crying my eyes out after Sam's call. How could I have been so stupid? I didn't know my own husband. I have been with him for many years, yet I still don't know him after all. Yes, I indeed chose Jack, but I thought Sam was a decent man, and we could still remain friends. But after his confession, there's no way I can look at his face again. He has destroyed all the love that was left for him, just like that.

Jack knocked on the door yet again, trying to get me to open it once more.

"Please, Isabel. Let me in," his voice was desperate now. "If you don't open this door, you leave me no choice but to knock it down," he said, pounding on the door harder.

I wanted the open the door and let him in. Let him hold me and tell me that everything will be okay. Let him lie to me and say all of this will end, but I know that's not true. I figured I need to distance myself from him, from everyone I love, because I wouldn't be here long. After I have seen all the plan details, the conversation William and I had. . . everything rushed inside my brain, bringing me to only one conclusion. *I have to do as William asks of me.*

"Just leave me alone," I said between sobs.

"Fuck," I heard him whisper on the other side. A little later, I heard something sliding against the door as if Jack gave up and sat down.

"Why are you pushing me away, baby?" he spoke softly.

I wanted to cry harder, but I held it in. As I didn't answer him, he spoke again.

"Why can't we just go back to how it used to be between us. Easy, calm, happy," Jack said.

The sadness in his voice almost broke me.

"Do you remember on your birthday when we went to the countryside, and we went for a bicycle ride? We were so happy, so close. There was nothing that could affect us then," Jack recalled.

It hurts remembering those great times with Jack, so I got up from the floor and washed my face.

"Things change, people change," I said as I opened the door.

Jack almost fell against my legs. He quickly got up and pulled me into my arms.

"That's okay. I still love you no matter how much you have been pushing me away. . ." he whispered and continued, "I won't let you go, no matter how bad you treat me sometimes, no matter what you say or do, I will never let you go," he said.

Jack and I always have this connection between us. We seem to know when something is wrong when the other person feels something - we sense each other's thoughts and feelings. I believe what he was saying to be true, but what he didn't know is that he has no choice but to let me go. I will have to do this for him and Lara. I know William said that he wants Lara to come, too, but I could never imagine a life for Lara when we are with William. I have decided that Jack will look after Lara with the help of Lizzy. Maybe Jack and Lizzy would have a chance? This thought made me cringe so much I rushed to embrace the toilet, and the food I ate came rushing out from my mouth.

Jack's hands were holding my hair out of the way, which he has been doing so many times lately.

"You need to rest. You can't get stressed anymore, Isabel. This will be bad for the baby and for you, too," he said kindly.

"I'm okay. It's nothing," I said, trying to look calm and unaffected.

"Just stop saying you are okay because you are clearly not," he said, frustrated with me.

He dragged me to bed and brought me a wet cloth, which he then placed it over my forehead. He moved a strand of hair away from my face before speaking again.

"What did Sam say for you to be so upset? You know you can trust me, baby. Maybe I can help."

I want to tell him so badly, but what for? What can he possibly say or do to make me feel less betrayed, less hurt?

"Nothing that affects you," I said.

By this time, Jack already looked annoyed and hurt by my statement. He looked down at his hands and said, "If you knew how hurtful you are when you say things like that, you would never utter them out."

He looked at me with his beautiful green eyes, the eyes I have fallen in love with, the first moment I say them. The eyes that will go away with me to the grave branded in my brain, my heart, and my soul.

"Isabel, I don't know what you are going through at the moment. You are keeping me at arms' length, and I can't say I'm okay with that but. . . I understand that sometimes we do things to protect the ones we care about. I can only assure you that I'm here. I'm not going anywhere. I'm going to make sure nothing will ever happen to you, Lara. . ." he puts his hand on my tummy carefully, softly. ". . . or our baby." This is the first time he spoke so lovingly about our baby.

"When I pushed you away, you never gave up on me, and I will never give up on us either. I promise." His words were like fire to my already scorched hear. Tears started to fall from my eyes, uninvited. How on earth will I be able to break this man's heart?

"Do you understand? No matter how it hurts hearing, you say such things, I will be here beside you. Always," he kissed me softly on the lips, and I wanted to sob but held them in instead.

He left the room without looking back. I know him well enough to know he was going to do something important. He made his mind up about something, and I can guess it has to do with getting in touch with William. I knew it would be useless, but I needed the time this thing will take for me to sort everything out. The first thing I did was write letters, one for Lizzy, one for my mum, one for Alex, one for my beautiful girl Lara, and the last one for Jack. My mum's letter was short, simple but told her everything I needed her to know.

Minha Mae Querida (My darling mother),
You brought me into this world with so much happiness but so much hardship. I want you to know that I appreciate everything you have ever done for me. For every beating you took from father in my stead, for every tear you shed because of my sorrows, for every night you missed because of me. I love you and want you to live life to the fullest, even though I'm not going to be with you in person my thoughts will always be, and I will carry you in my heart.
With much love,
Da tua querida filha
(from your darling daughter)
Isabel

Lizzy's was a bit longer as I needed to give her instructions and tell her everything she will need to know to support Jack in raising Lara.

My dear, Sister Lizzy,
There is so much I need to say to you, but there isn't enough paper in the world that could fit all that I feel and want to say, so I will try and keep to the most important facts.
I love you as my own flesh and blood. You have always been there for me without hesitation or doubts. You taught me a lot all these years, and one thing was that we could survive anything if we do it together. Well, now I'm teaching you something new. We can survive anything even if we are apart because no matter how far away we are from each other, we carry each other in our hearts.

What I'm about to ask you is not going to be simple or easy, but it's something I can't ask from anyone else except you. I don't see anyone more capable or more fitting to help me with this. I have to give myself to William as his mistress. I need to keep everyone I care about safe, and the only way is to do this. So, I'm hoping and trusting that Jack accepts what I ask of him, to take care of Lara as his own. I need you to be there for them. They will need you now more than ever, and I need you to be the mother I cannot be for Lara. Don't let her hate me, please. I couldn't bear if any of you hated me for this. I know Jack won't give up easily on finding a way to get me back, and I won't ask him to because I still hope in my heart that one day, very soon, he will find a way to end this nightmare. But if he loses hope and wants to move on with his life, please let him be. I want his happiness, and if he finds it with someone else, I can live with that.

Before I say goodbye, I just want you to know that I hope you find love again. I know it is possible to find that special someone again, you just need to open up your heart and you will find it when you least expect it - just like how I found Jack.

I wish I would say see you later. Unfortunately, it's good-bye for now. I love you more than words can say.

Be safe, my sweet Lizzy.
Your best friend and sister,
Isabel

My tears blinded me after these two letters, but I still had a few more to write, so I pushed it on. What do you say to your own daughter when you will disappear from her life. I have been the only person who has been constantly with her since the day she was born. I was lost for words for a while. I couldn't explain why, but I couldn't let her know how hard this was for me and how I wished to be with her.

My beautiful girl,

If you are reading this letter, it means I'm unable to be with you contrary to what I have always promised and for that I'm truly sorry. I know that you are confused, scared, and hurt, but it'll all pass with time, my sweet pea. I just want you to know that I'm no longer going to be there for you not because I don't want to, but because I can't.

Please be kind and patient with Jack, he will be as upset as you about my absence, and he'll need your help and love, so find comfort in his cuddles for me.

I know you are a star already, but soon, you'll become an even bigger star than you already are. Never be afraid to reach for your dreams, and remember I will always be thinking of you, my beautiful girl.

With all my love and soul,
Mummy

Alex's letter was next. This one I knew exactly what I needed to write, so I went straight to the point.

Dear Alex,
First of all, I'm sorry for not listening to you, and thank you for your hard work and dedication to keeping us all safe. I know you are upset and disappointed with my behaviour, but I had no choice. I know that, and you know that too by now. I gave you more time to find a way to bring William and the whole mafia down.

Please don't forget the Russian mafia is also involved, so they have to be considered in whatever plan you can come up with. If there is a way, I know you will find it, I'm sure of it. Please make sure Jack doesn't do anything stupid; we both know how hot-headed he can get. Could you also ensure Sam has a good life? I have transferred three million pounds to an offshore account. I have put all the details together with this letter - please ensure he has them and make sure he helps the woman and child in Venezuela he left behind.

Finally, please make sure all the people I love are safe in my absence, even though William promised he wouldn't harm anyone, I would still feel better if I know you are there to protect them. Even if Jack dismisses you at any point, I have set up a wage to be transferred every month to you.

Once more, thank you for your dedication. Be safe, and keep them safe for me.

With much love,

Isabel

My final letter was written with so much effort, I couldn't muster the courage to tell him everything I wanted to tell him. I didn't know if he would ever forgive me for this. I was afraid to bid goodbye. I was hopeful that he would find a way to get me back, but I was also doubtful that he could live with me after getting me back. In reality, I didn't believe he could ever look at me the same way as he did and do now. Not after knowing, I have been with someone else, even if it was against my will, this is something a couple rarely overcomes.

The circumstances are different this case than the normal affair situations, but that is what I would be doing. I will become someone's toy, sadly. I will be an object for pleasuring a sick bastard. What man can forgive or forget that?

In the end, I told him what he needed to know, but not a lot more. I couldn't even think of his reaction when reading my letter. It was too difficult for me to cope. By the time I shut my eyes to sleep, my heart felt like it was completely broken and beyond fixing. I was tired of crying; every part of my body hurt, my tummy was so sore even after taking the medication for the pain Dr. Shelly has prescribed, the soreness didn't fade. Maybe it was all in my head, but I felt completely broken inside and out.

CHAPTER 18

William

I smiled at my mobile phone's screen when I saw who it was. I have been waiting for his call longer than I thought it would take, but he didn't fail.

"Mr. Reed, to what I owe the pleasure?" I said as a manner of answering the call.

"It's Jack, please. Mr. Reed is my father," he said calmly.

"My apologies, Jack. What can I do for you?" I said, enjoying this little game.

"Let us cut out the bullshit. You know exactly why I'm calling. We need to meet and discuss the Winter's family issue." He sounded almost bored like he wasn't worried as I thought he was.

"Oh? And what would the issue be?" I feigned to understand what he wants.

Jack let out a sigh of frustration, "Look, William, what we need to discuss can't be done over the phone. Let's arrange a meeting."

I laughed on the inside that his cool facade is starting to tremble and fall.

"Sure, my friend. Just tell me where and when, and we can have a chat," I said, smiling.

"Tomorrow, 8 pm, Italian Gardens in Hyde Park," he said.

I see, he wants a public place. This only means that he's worried.

"I'll be there. Oh Jack, how is Isabel feeling?" I said, teasing him.

The silence that followed after had me chuckling. "Give her my regards, will you?" I said before disconnecting the call.

I laughed out loud when I ended the call. This is going to be so much fun. When I tell him what I want, after all, it will throw him off, and he won't be able to hold back. This is the best opportunity to hurt him. *Yes, that'll be nice.*

I never used to be this cruel, really. But after the upbringing I had, I think anyone would. . . become beyond insane. I wanted so much to keep out of the family business. Unfortunately, with the family name I have, and after my brother's death, I knew it would be impossible. I'm not like my late brother. He was a true *boss,* but I had to adapt pretty quickly. I killed, yes, more than I can count. My brother used to kill because he enjoyed it as much as my father did. I feel that we can still keep order and loyalty and not just out of fear among members of the Crown. This is how I have operated, and it works pretty well.

I thought of Isabel, of the moment she would become mine. The way I would get her was not exactly ideal, but at least, she would be mine. I would make sure that she would be treated like a queen, and her baby would be mine, too.

I tried to imagine a little baby in her arms, next to me, and it made my heart warm. Even though it's not mine, I believe I could take it in as my own.

Her sickness, her cancer, is making her weak. But she's a strong woman. I know she will bite the offer I have for her on treatment surrounded by renowned specialists. I promised her no harm, would come to anyone she loves, and I intend to keep it. What I'm worried about is that fucking Russian bastard who soon will be my father-in-law, Demyan. I will probably have to move the wedding forward to show my loyalty. Demyan loves to show his authority, but I believe he won't oppose me, bringing Isabel to my side. This will make a show of powerful, I take what I want when I want.

I'll make sure she has always one of my men around her. Probably Finley just to show Demyan this is purely business. My phone buzzed again, and I knew who it was immediately.

"Hi, Ma," I answered my mother's call, and hear her quiet weeping in the background.

I knew something was wrong. "What is it, Ma?" I asked.

"Your father. . ." she said. Dread came over me.

"His heart stopped again, and Dr. Patel says that this time, it has done so much damage that she thinks he has very little time left. Come home, son. Come home before he leaves us," she managed to convince me.

"I'm on my way, Ma," I said, already leaving my office and nodding to Philip and Tommy to follow me.

I knew this day would come. My old man has had a few heart failures in the past, and the damage it causes every time it happens is unfixable. Even with the best specialists on payroll, he can't be fixed.

"Take me home, Tommy. And fast," I commanded him.

The ride home was quiet and nervous. I was tapping my leg continuously. Soon enough, the gates from the family estate open up, and the car comes to a stop in the front of the stone-pillar entrance of the house. I immediately jumped out and rushed inside. I found all my family around my old man's bed weeping, and I felt my own eyes sting, but I swallowed my pain and made sure there were no tears in my eyes before approaching him.

"I need a minute alone with him," I said in a rough, hard voice.

My mother shooed everyone from the room. Before she left, she gave me a warm kiss on my cheek. I didn't budge to embrace her or show any emotion. Since I had become the head of the family business, I showed no one any emotions at all, including my mother, whom I was close with before. She understood I had to do this to protect myself from situations like this. When the time comes that I lose someone I loved, I would be able to deal with it easily.

I stepped forward once the bedroom door was closed shut. The only people who remained in the room were my father and I. I looked at him, and I could hear his laboured breathing while his eyes were shut. His face was white as a ghost, heck, he looked more dead than alive.

"Father," I whispered, and I knelt next to the bed and held his frail hand.

My father slowly opened his eyes. I bet it was painful because he whizzed out, "My son."

"Shhh. . . Don't talk. Save your energy. I'm here," I said gently.

He shook his head slightly, "I need. . . I need to tell you. . ." he breathed out almost like he can't die before speaking to me.

He pulled me closer to him and said, "I never. . . told you how proud. . . how proud I am of you. Keep them safe. No matter what. . . no matter what. . . put the. . . family first," he said, gasping.

Of course, this is the legacy he leaves for me. "I will, father. I promise no harm will come to any one of the Hamiltons'. We will rule as we have been doing for so many years. I will have a son, and our legacy will continue," I said strongly.

My father smiled at me and patted my cheek lightly, closing his eyes, and I knew. . . I knew he was slipping. He was ready to go now that I made my promises. I wanted to cry. I wanted to bring him back. I didn't want to take the full responsibility he left me with. I wasn't ready yet. I wasn't ready to become the official head of the family, as well as the Crown. I kissed his forehead as if bidding goodbye.

"Goodbye, father. See you soon," I said before getting up, straightening my suit and wrist cufflinks.

I opened the bedroom door and looked at my mother, who understood right away that my father has passed away. She rushed in, weeping, and my little sister hugged me tightly also crying softly. I patted her in the back before I grabbed her by the shoulders and looked at her.

"There is no point in crying, little sis. You know he would find it weak, and it would not please him," I said, trying to hide the pain of seeing my sister hurt.

She nodded and tried to compose herself.

"Good. Now, I'll be downstairs in the office to sort the funeral arrangements, in case anyone asks."

She nodded once more and spoke, "You are truly our father's son."

The way she spoke had me felt that she didn't like what I said and the way I talked. I know she hated the person who I have become. So was I, but I just had to deal with it. I looked at her briefly before walking away.

On my way, I saw Philip and Tommy, who said their condolences. I dismissed them as they spoke, letting them know I was not interested.

"Can you make sure Frank gets the news and deal with the media, please. I don't want any journalists snooping around here at the estate or with any family member, understood?" I said sternly.

"Of course, boss," Philip replied before turning on his heels and rushing out of the office.

After four fucking hours of arranging everything for the funeral, I thought I had time to rest, but my phone has been receiving a lot of messages from people who want to say their condolences. Shortly after that, flowers were starting to come in with little cards attached to them. I felt bad as I missed my father. My chest tightened as I remember him in my head. Sure, he was ruthless and unforgiving, but at home, he was a great family man. He didn't really cuddle us or kissed us, but he was there during our important events such as football and ballet. Any game we got in, he never missed a chance to see us. He also taught us a lot, not just about business but also mundane things like riding a bike, driving, shooting, and a lot more.

I got up from the desk and walked to the window. I contemplated. I imagined Isabel by my side at this moment, her beautiful petit frame around me comforting me during this hard time. I let myself imagine how she would say how much she loves me and kissing me softly to try and erase my pain. Suddenly, a knock woke me up from my daydream.

"Boss, Miss Erika is here to see you."

I let out a sigh of frustration, not wanting to deal with her right now. I had no choice, so I nodded at Philip to let her in.

"Darling!!!" Erika's squeaky, annoying voice came from behind me. I braced myself, trying not to be annoyed at her.

I turned just in time, her hugging me close to her. To anyone's eyes looking at us, they would say she loves me very much. But I know for a fact that she doesn't give a fuck about me. She's a great actress who knows how to behave in our world.

"Erika," I said, patting her back slightly.

"I'm so sorry about your poor father," she said with a hint of sarcasm.

Erika cupped my face with one hand and brought her lips to mine. I have never felt so disgusted, so I let myself think of Isabel's golden eyes, and I let out a little moan. I felt Erika's lips stretch into a smile over my own, thinking I was actually into her. She let her hands roam my chest going lower, and reached out for my belt. Before she unbuckled me, I held her hand firmly.

"Let us not get carried away," I said, stepping back and dropping into the desk chair.

Erika's eyes were sparkling with mischief. She loves playing games on me.

"I couldn't wait to see again, my love. When daddy gave me the terrible news, I rushed right over. This must be very difficult for all of the family," she says, moving closer to me, leaning her backside right on the desk and putting one hand on the desk to support herself and the other on my shoulder rubbing it gently. Isabel once more popped into my mind. *Not for long now,* I told myself. *She will be by my side soon enough.*

"What is it you are thinking about, William?" Erika asked with a seductive tone. I must have let my emotions show when thinking about Isabel.

"Nothing you can help me with, love," I told her, smirking.

"Oh, I bet I could help. You know, it has been proven that sex can cure almost anything, and it's great for tension relief," she whispered in my ear.

I have to admit she was right. I looked at her, thinking if I should actually fuck her and get it over with, but. . . something was tugging me not to do it. It could be that Demyan would put a bullet in my head just as he has done to my brother if I fucked Erika.

"I heard that, too," I said, turning a little her way and putting my hand on her thighs and running ever so slowly upwards toward her *vagina* but I stopped just shy of it.

"You see, my dilemma is that I'm your fiance, and I respect you and your father too much that I don't want to do anything to you that might also upset him," I said, looking into her eyes, telling her what she wanted to hear.

"Oh, I wouldn't tell a soul," she said with a smirk, lying through her teeth.

She would definitely tell everyone just to make trouble. I know this beforehand, so I won't fuck her like she expects me to. Her family and ours got into a huge fight for what her dad did to Samuel, but my father values the alliance too much, so he made another deal.

"I'm happy to wait for the wedding, my love. We can both look forward to it even more fervently. Don't you think?" I said smirking, just as she was moments ago.

She let out a sigh and got off from the desk, and moved to the burgundy leather sofa in the corner.

"Fine, have it your way. . . for now," she said, looking at me like she was undressing me.

I won't lie, my dick was straining a little. After all, a man has his needs. Having a woman throwing herself at you will always stir something badly. But when the time comes for me to actually fuck her, I think I will have to think of Isabel the entire time. The thought of Isabel again was too much. I had to do something about how turned on I was right now. I excused myself while I dealt with myself in my bedroom en-suit.

Once I got there, all I could think about was her scent, her beautiful innocent eyes, her plump lips, fuck. I took all my clothes off and turned on the shower. I might as well do this in the shower, I thought to myself. I held on my dick, stroking it slow at first, imagining Isabel kissing it, licking it. . . and then sucking it. I was throbbing as I increased the pace, imagining slamming into her real hard from behind, getting in and out faster, slapping her bottom while riding her hard. The thought of her screaming my name did it.

I came hard, moaning.

"Fuck. Just the thought of you do this to me," I said out loud as if she was right next to me. I rested my back against the tiled wall in the shower letting the hot water soothe my muscles and the relieved feeling it brought me in this moment felt great.

She'll soon be mine, and I'll have her for real.

CHAPTER 19

Jack

When Alex relayed to me Sam's call to Isabel, her behaviour made sense. I couldn't believe Sam was so stupid, so careless. Isabel is hurting so badly, and I couldn't do anything about that apart of being here for her. The mood in the house was somber. Alex has been very vague lately; I feel like he's trying to avoid me. I can't put my finger on it, but my instinct tells me that something is going on, so I called him up on this.

"Jack, you called me?"

"Alex, something is going on, and I want to know what it is," I said in a firm voice. Alex let a sigh escape and pinched the bridge in his nose.

"Jack, this is a mess. Sam wants to give himself up, Isabel. . ." he stopped himself, rubbing his hand over his face.

"Isabel, what?" I shouted. I knew she was hiding something from me, and Alex was on it, too.

"For fuck's sake, speak!" I shouted again.

"I'm worried that she might do something stupid," Alex said.

"Like what?" I asked, trying to keep my cool. Alex takes a sit on the chair in front of my desk.

"I think she might give herself to William," he finally said.

Wait, what did he just say? Alex must have seen the confusion on my face because he carried on continuing to explain.

"That day in the museum, William told Isabel what he wants," Alex said.

"He told her what he wants, and Sam is not it," he continued.

I had a bad feeling about what he was going to say next, but he tried simplifying it to me.

"How much?" I asked. I prayed he wanted money because it would be easier. Obviously, William wanted the money he lost, but Alex shook his head.

"He doesn't want money," Alex said sadly.

If it wasn't money, then what is it? I thought of Alex's comment earlier.

"No. . . You can't mean he wants. . . No," I gasped while shaking my head furiously.

Alex closed his eyes briefly and said, "He wants Isabel for himself."

"You fucking bastard! And you just told me this *now?*" I said, fuming and screaming. I shot to my feet and went around Alex grabbing his t-shirt and bringing him closer to me.

"How could I trust you with her safety? How could you not tell me this?"

Despite my outburst, Alex didn't seem to have been fazed.

"Isabel made me promise I wouldn't tell you. I only agreed because she promised me she wouldn't do anything before we have tried the plan we agreed on," he says, looking at me dead in the eye, but I didn't remove my grip right away.

I let go of him slowly, trying to let go of my anger a little, too. I knew whatever he demanded made Isabel very afraid, but not in a million years I thought she was the one William wants. It just didn't make sense to me.

"You betrayed my trust, Alex," I told him. Maybe I was being too hard on Alex but withheld a piece of vital information that could put Isabel in danger was out of order.

"No, Jack. I'm telling you now because this is the right time. I truly believed Isabel was going to wait and try the plan first, but now. . ." Alex paused.

"Now what?"

"I think she hasn't found other ways. She thinks William is too powerful to be caught."

I was extremely angry and frustrated at this point.

"Where is she now?" I asked worryingly.

"Relax, she's still asleep. I just checked on her before coming here to see you."

"We have to prevent her from doing something stupid. She can't give herself in, he will kill her," I said.

Alex seemed to not agree with me, so I asked, "What are you thinking, Alex?"

"William wouldn't kill her. She specifically said he wanted her to be his mistress. That he would give her everything she would ever want and would never harm anyone she loves."

Now I see how she would want to give herself to him. She would want to protect me, Lara, Lizzy, and everyone else. Now I understand how dangerous leaving her alone could be. I dashed for the door and sprinted the stairs steps until I reached Isabel's bedroom. I frantically pulled the bed covers off and panicked when I didn't find her in bed. I heard heaving noises from the en-suite toilet and rushed to it. I found Isabel rinsing her mouth on the basin and looked up to me through the mirror. She realised that I knew. She lowered her eyes and hung her head.

"Jack. . ." she starts before turning towards me.

"How can you think I would allow you to leave me and become his mistress?!" I growled more than ever.

She crossed her arms and let a loud sigh out. "There isn't really any other choice, Jack. Believe me, I thought of everything."

"Stop! That's not even a fucking choice, Isabel!" I shouted at her.

She looked back at me angrily. "You think I would even consider this if there was any other choice? There isn't any other way, Jack!" she shouted back at me.

With her outburst, she wobbled, putting her hand on her head. Just before she passed out, I grabbed her preventing her head from hitting the basin.

"Alex!" I screamed.

"Yes?" he says, rushing from the bedroom door minutes later.

"I'm in here," I shouted.

"Get Dr. Shelly! Hurry!" By this time, Isabel has passed out in my arms, looking white as a sheet. I picked her up and laid her on the bed. I checked her breathing and grabbed a wet cloth putting it on her forehead.

She slowly came to her senses and tried to get up from the bed.

"Don't move. You just fainted. Try to relax, okay?" I managed to say. My hands were trembling. I felt stupid for shouting at her like that, I forgot how fragile she was because of her condition. She must have sensed my guilt because she lifted her hand gently to my cheek.

"I'm okay, Jack. This is normal. After I throw up, I usually feel weak," she said, trying to reassure me which it didn't. I shook my head but didn't say a word further. I felt so fucking frustrated for not being able to cope with the situation. It is completely out of hand; we can't keep this up for much longer. We have to catch William and put him under custody, and we can't go wrong with this plan.

After 30 minutes, Dr. Shelly came over and checked Isabel. "I want to admit her into the hospital to keep an eye on her. She needs fluids, and she seems to have an infection. I need to run tests to make sure nothing is serious.

I could see that even Dr. Shelly was worried. "We'll bring her to the hospital right away," I said.

"I'll call the hospital to set everything up," he said, picking up his mobile phone.

I nodded and went to get a night bag to put together the things I knew she would need or want. I went about it without talking to Isabel. To be honest, I don't even know what to say to her. We couldn't discuss the issue at hand as she wasn't well enough, and I didn't want to say anything that might upset her, so I kept quiet and focused on what needed to be done. It was probably best for her that she stayed in the hospital. It would prevent her from making the biggest mistake in her life, by giving herself over to William.

I could feel the weight of her gaze on me the whole time, but I tried not to look at her. It pained me the way she looked at me and the thoughts she could have thought about her plan.

When we arrived in the hospital, we were all set up in a single room. Nurses were coming in and going out with laboratory accessories such as test tubes, blood pressure machine, thermometers, and a lot more. They put an IV on Isabel after a while. I was standing in a corner seeing all the movement around when Dr. Shelly came in.

"How are you doing and feeling?" he asked Isabel kindly.

"I have been better, thank you," she says in a small voice.

"You have a viral infection. Nothing to worry too much about since the antibiotics I have prescribed will cure you of this. But I want you to be critical of who goes in and out. Make sure you won't be in direct contact with anyone, as someone could be bringing bacteria that will only exacerbate your immune system. Understood?" Isabel nodded in agreement.

"We'll be doing a scan in a little while, too. Just to make sure the little one is doing well, too," Dr. Shelly told us both.

"How long will she be here, Doctor?" I wondered. I could see that Isabel was disappointed, but I moved my eyes to Dr. Shelly.

"Until I'm sure the infection is gone, I would say about 3 to 4 days at most," he said.

I nodded happily. That would give me time to meet William, and she will be out of harm's way. When she comes home, everything will be over, and we will move forward with our lives at long last. I wanted to stay with Isabel at the hospital, but she insisted I come home, so I did. I was looking at a picture of us three in my office. Lara, Isabel, and I look so happy, so carefree in the photo. That seemed to be ages ago, but it was taken only five months ago. I loosened my blue tie and undid the first button of my white shirt. Later that day, it took me over an hour to put Lara to sleep, but eventually, she got tired, so she gave up and closed her eyes. Isabel was still in my thoughts during that time. I was both relieved and worried about Isabel. Her health was becoming something we both should be worried about. Since she's pregnant, she must be taken care of because anything she feels, catches, the baby also feels the same. Everything I ever wanted is within my grasp but yet only held by a thread.

I rubbed my face with my hands and tried to focus on the details I have in front of me to meet William tomorrow night. The team has been set up with the best of the best, or so they tell me. Alex is working out in the gym now as part of his routine, preparing for a major operation. My doubts started to creep again, but I quickly cleared them away. *It will work, and I will take care of my beautiful family. I will take care of Isabel for the rest of our lives, and I will love our children unconditionally. I promise that.*

The day to meet William has come. I visited Isabel earlier at the hospital, and she was as quiet as yesterday, but her eyes were even sadder. Before I left, she cupped my face bringing her lips to mine with so much enthusiasm tasting me with her tongue with a desperation that took me by surprise. She ended the kiss and brought her forehead to mine before saying, "I love you. Be careful and be safe, my love." She gazed into my eyes, and I felt sad.

I made sure that she wasn't going anywhere, and no one can come close to her. I had Luke guard her, but I felt different this time, so I asked Alex to call Luke and confirm that Isabel was still in the room. Alex confirmed shortly, but I still felt uneasy. I couldn't put my finger on what was this uneasy feeling, but since Alex assured me and convinced me to focus on the situation, I was in at the moment, as the next hour would bring peace to my family and me.

"We have eyes on the target, everyone. They're just passing the fountain and are coming towards you, Jack," I heard Agent Simons telling me in my earpiece.

I spotted William coming towards the bench where I was sitting. I sat there with ease, or at least I thought to myself. He was wearing light blue Chino trousers and a button-down shirt with a light blue scarf around his thick neck. He was also covered with a long cream jacket and looked like a professor.

William sits next to me, looking all relaxed. "Good evening, Jack," he says, looking at the park.

"I was wondering if you wouldn't turn up," I told him.

"Oh, I'm a little late, all right, but I want to be here," he says with a smirk on his face.

I looked at him a little longer thinking if he had ulterior motives, but can't seem to figure out if he was just careless sitting next to me.

"I believe we are here to discuss the Winters' dilemma?" he asked me, bringing his arm over the back of the bench and turning my way slightly.

"What do you want me to do to make sure no harm will come to anyone, William?" I asked.

"You already know what I want," he immediately chuckled back.

"So, you admit that you want to hurt the Winters' family?" I asked him, trying to get him to admit.

"Keep calm, Jack. Don't bite the bait," I heard Alex on my earpiece.

William didn't answer my question, so I pushed forward.

"You know what you asked for is never going to happen. So tell me how much money do you want, and you shall have it," I said, stalling as part of the plan.

William laughs at what I said but didn't comment right away. "Jack, do you really think I need or want money from you? Where I am right now, I really don't need anything."

Bastard. He knows this is a trap.

"Cut the bullshit, William. It doesn't suit you," I said with conviction.

"What bullshit, Jack? I'm just telling the truth," he said, looking straight at me.

I wanted to punch him now and hurt him even though I have never hurt anyone before.

"How is Sam?" he suddenly asked out of the blue.

If looks could kill, I could have killed right him now.

"He's safe," I told him.

"Oh, he's always been safe," he said with a huge grin. "Don't you know Jack that this was never about Sam?"

A realisation dawned on me: he planned this from the beginning even before Sam came into the picture. Could it be that he wanted Isabel all along?

William must have seen the realisation in my expression because he stood up and straightened his cufflinks. His phone started to ring to which he answered with a smirk on his face. I was about to lose my cool when a voice suddenly caught me in the earpiece, "Keep him talking, Jack. We need more. We can't bring him in like this. We have nothing," Agent Simons instructed me.

"Oh, perfect. Let her know I will be with her shortly," William said, talking to his phone.

"We haven't finished discussing the issue," I said, getting up close to him.

He chuckled slightly amused of the situation, "I beg to differ. I have what I always wanted, Jack."

As I was about to lose my control, he blurted, "She came on her own free will."

I lunged at him with all I had in one swift punch to his face. I hit him in the jaw, but the second punch didn't reach him as he was too fast. He laughed, and two men came walking beside him. I felt Alex holding my arm.

"It was a pleasure to have this little chat, Jack. We should do it again soon. And don't worry, I'll take care of her - better than you ever did," William said with a smug smile.

"You won't get away with this, William. I will make sure to put you behind bars where you belong!" I shouted at him.

"I look forward to seeing you try, my friend," he said, chuckling out of the park.

"Fuck. Isabel," I told Alex, but he was already on the phone.

"Luke isn't picking up. I'll call the hospital," Alex said, worry written on his face.

I was anxious, agitated, and I was running through the park to reach my car. Hopefully, I won't be too late. I took out the earpiece ignoring now Agent Simons. I couldn't believe Isabel would do that to me. I need to get to her before William does.

"Jack! Jack!" Alex reached me in seconds and grabbed me by my shoulders. When he spoke, I felt myself roaring and pushing against him, not believing what was happening.

"Isabel is gone. Luke was found in the toilet of the hospital completely knocked out," Alex said.

She did it, she left me.

CHAPTER 20

Isabel

My goodbye kiss to Jack lingered on my lips. I could still see the worry in his eyes because deep down, he knew it was a goodbye kiss even if he didn't want to admit it. I know the plan won't work; he knows it won't work, thus leaving me only one option.

I picked up my phone from the table beside my bed in the hospital room. This is probably the most difficult call I will make in my life. The phone rings, and he picks up on the second ring.

"Isabel, what a lovely surprise," I hear William's voice through the receiver.

"I made my decision," I said, determined to get the situation over with. William's silence compelled me to answer him without him having to ask.

"I'm yours but with few conditions," I say, looking at the stuffed teddy bear Jack dropped earlier for me. I was reading the writing on the toy's belly, and it bore the words, "I LOVE YOU."

"I won't bring my little girl with me. She stays with Jack. Everyone I care for, every single one of them is in no way to be harmed under any circumstances," I said strongly.

"Lastly, when my baby is born and if I decide to give him up and hand him to his father, you will allow it," I added.

There was a long deafening silence that followed after. I was sure that William didn't like the idea.

"Anything else?" he asked in a low, sad voice.

"We'll take everything at my pace. This. . . this relation-ship," I said gulping. It was fucking hard to see this relationship the way it should be, but I needed to make sure he trusted me, so I still have a chance to find a way back to my family. I heard a long sigh before he spoke again.

"Agreed," he says sternly.

"I'm at the hospital in Chelsea. Can you pick me up?" I asked. I suddenly remembered that Luke was outside, so I quickly told William about it.

"I can't leave my room. I have someone by the door who's guarding me."

William chuckled a bit which I was annoyed, "Don't worry, little Isabel. Someone will pick you up, and there won't be any obstacles."

I was worried about what he said that he might harm Luke. I didn't want him to get hurt. "Don't you dare hurt Luke. Do you understand?"

William let out a frustrated sigh, "Isabel, I promise he won't be killed or seriously injured. Now, is that enough?"

I guess it could be worst, he could just shoot Luke. So I agree to his terms knowing Luke won't be too badly hurt.

"Yes."

"Get yourself ready. Someone will pick you up tonight," he ended the call.

I scrolled down, looking for Sofia's number in my contact list. I had to call her twice before she picked up.

"Hello?"

"Hi, Sofia. How are you?"

"I'm okay, Isabel. How about you? Do you need some-thing?" she asked. She must think it was so strange for me to call her while I'm still at the hospital.

"I'm a little better, thank you. Listen, I need your help with something. Can you please go to my bedroom and check on the bedside table. There are a bunch of letters with names written on them, they are on the second drawer of my dressing area. Can you make sure they reach the right people please."

There was a short silence from Sofia before she spoke. "Isabel, is everything okay? You don't sound very well. Maybe when you are back from the hospital, you can give them yourself. . ." she said quietly.

She must have sensed something was up. Of course, she knew what was up, but she didn't know all the details.

"Sofia, I have no one I can ask this from. You can leave Jack's letter on the desk of his office, and give everyone else's after he read his. Can you do that for me, please?" I asked with a little urgency.

"Yes, of course, Isabel. I'll do that for you," she said.

"Thank you, Sofia. Please take care of yourself and make sure my little girl eats well."

"Isabel, what's this about *querida*? You are scaring me. Where are you going? What is happening?" she asked urgently.

I felt my eyes were stinging as I was about to cry. "I have to go now. Thank you and take care!" I said, ending the call and sobbing quietly into the pillow so Luke wouldn't notice.

After the nurse came in to check on me at 8:30 pm, I rushed to get dressed, and as I picked my overnight bag and Jack's teddy bear, I heard the door open. I froze, and I was panicking as I thought the nurse missed something. Suddenly, a gruff voice behind me demanded, "Isabel, let's go."

I looked behind my shoulder and saw the man from the surveillance pictures Alex showed me before. It was Finley, the one who works for William. He had a serious look on his face, and he was looking between me and the corridor.

"Come on, move. William will be waiting," he says in a rush. I moved as fast I could, trying to keep up with his long strides. I noticed that the nurse's stations were empty. I found it strange, but I didn't bother asking Finley about it because I was too scared to find out the answer. We took the stairs to the car park. We entered the car that was waiting for us. Finley helped me climb up into the back seat. He took my overnight bag, and as he was about to take the teddy bear, I grabbed it from him and held it tight to my chest.

"No! I'll take this," I say, worried he might take it away from me. It was the only thing I had from Jack, and I wouldn't let go of it.

Finley closed the door and got into the front passenger seat. "Let's go," he told the driver. He picked up his phone and then said, "We have her. We are on our way to the house."

I assumed he was talking to William, but I felt really scared. I know he was with Jack now, and as soon as Jack finds out about this from William, he would do something stupid that would cost his life. But I know that William wouldn't harm him, he promised me.

"We are going to the house. William will meet us there in a little while," Finley told me. He was looking at me, I wonder if he was trying to find something out.

Moments later, we have arrived at the house. The house he was referring to earlier wasn't a house. It was an estate just outside the city. The drive from the gate to the front door was long, and the entrance to the front door was grand and imposing. Finley opens the car door, and I carefully stepped out careful not to fall on my knees as I was feeling dizzy and weak. He must have seen it in my face because he held my arm gently as he took me inside.

"James, is the south wing ready?" Finley asked the butler as we were walking inside.

"It is, Sir. Is Mr. Hamitlon joining you?" the elegant butler asked.

"He's on his way. Can you bring some tea, please?" Finley asked.

"Most certainly, Sir."

The butler left, and Finley took me upstairs. I can't help myself admiring the sophistication and glamorous decor of the place. When we arrived at the south wing, I was taken aback from the sheer size of the place. There were exactly eight doors - eight double doors. We entered one of those doors, and it was a huge bedroom. It had a four-poster bed, a long, antique ottoman, a window seat, a little sitting area by the other window, it was massive.

"This is your room. Have a seat, please," Finley politely asked me, which threw me off a bit. He doesn't seem to be as mean as I pictured him to be in my head.

"Why are you nice to me?" I asked in a small voice.

Finley chuckled, "Well, I kind of have to be. I'll be your escort from now on." He saw the confusion I expressed, so he said, "I'll let the boss explain it to you."

He gestured me to sit on a beautiful light pink chair in the waiting area. I looked around to take in all the gorgeous decor. The colour scheme is light pink and gold. They even have a vase of fresh flowers that match the colours on the coffee table in front of me.

This is where I'll be living then. I just hope it'll only be for a short period of time. I don't know how I'll cope without my little girl. Oh god. My baby girl. With the thought of her, tears fell from my eyes. I swiped at them fast as I turned away from Finley. I didn't want him to see me like that because he might think I was weak.

"Where's the bathroom, please?" I asked.

Finley got up and turned to a long wall on the other side of the bed and presses something. Suddenly, the hidden door opened. Without a word, I quickly walked and got into the bathroom. I didn't know how long I was inside crying, but I knew I had to calm down, get this over with, and face the new challenge of my life. I washed my face, fixed my hair, and came into the bedroom.

When I came back, I didn't find Finley anywhere in the room, but there was someone else. Someone I was dreading to see. It was William.

"I'm sorry for not being here when you arrived. But as you know. . ." he said while looking me from across the room next to one of the large windows. He seemed a bit tense, so I became worried something might have happened to Jack. William might have read the worry written all over my face because he took his hands from his chino trousers' pockets and came closer to me.

"Jack's fine," he said gently.

When he came closer, I saw a mark on his cheek. I wondered if Jack did this to him. He might have noticed I was looking at it.

"I told you I wouldn't hurt him, no matter what. I kept my promise, for you," he said, looking into my eyes and then to my lips.

I took one step back and looked around, not knowing what to do or say. William was just there looking at me like he wanted to eat me alive. It made me even more uncomfortable. I sat on the chair and took a sip of the tea that was prepared for me. I drank, but my tummy hurt I felt like the room was tilting and moving. My chest hurts so bad that Jack's eyes came to my mind. I miss his lips, our last kiss, his proposal, our passionate nights together. This is too much for me, and the pain was indescribable. I dropped the cup that I was holding and felt like I needed to rest my head on hands. I felt Williams' hands over mine, and I slowly removed my hands away. He puts his large hand so carefully over my forehead.

"You're burning up. Let's get you into bed, and I'll have a doctor over in just a little while," William said.

All I could think about at the moment was how Jack would be feeling and what he's going through right now because I left. William made me leave, I wanted to slap his hand away. I wanted to lash out and call him all the worst names there are, but I couldn't do it. I tried so hard not to faint, but the dizziness came crashing fast, and I just felt myself dropping forwards. The coffee table was the last thing I saw.

To be continued. . .

Lightning Source UK Ltd.
Milton Keynes UK
UKHW020806160620
364898UK00003B/107